Best
Pub Walks in the Dark Peak

Les Lumsdon and Martin Smith

Published by Sigma Leisure – an imprint of
Sigma Press, 5 Alton Road, Wilmslow, Cheshire SK9 5DY, England.

British Library Cataloguing in Publication Data
A CIP record for this book is available from the British Library.

ISBN: 1-85058-815-5

Typesetting and Design by: Sigma Press, Wilmslow, Cheshire.

Cover photograph: The Navigation Inn, Buxworth

Maps: Bute Cartographics. Reproduced by permission of Ordnance Survey on behalf of The Controller of Her Majesty's Stationery Office, © Crown Copyright 2004 100032058

Printed by: Progress Press, Malta

Disclaimer: the information in this book is given in good faith and is believed to be correct at the time of publication. No responsibility is accepted by either the author or publisher for errors or omissions, or for any loss or injury howsoever caused. Only you can judge your own fitness, competence and experience. Do not rely solely on sketch maps for navigation: we strongly recommend the use of appropriate Ordnance Survey (or equivalent) maps.

Contents

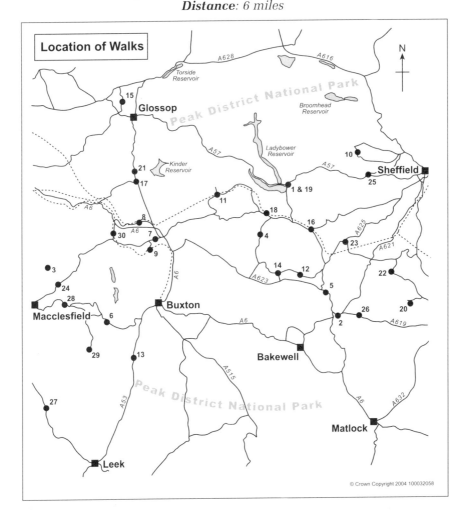

The Peak District and its Pubs

Given the outstanding beauty of its landscape, plus its history, culture and accessibility, it is hardly surprising that the Peak District is so well walked. The network of paths and tracks is, for the most part, in good order – a bonus for those visitors whose local paths may be poorly maintained or obstructed.

The Peak District lies at the southern end of the Pennines – the "backbone of England" and contains some of the finest gritstone scenery in the country. This is the area covered by this book. The gritstone edges and the high moors of Kinder Scout and Bleaklow, with their characteristic cloaks of dark peat and heather that are beloved of the rambler. It was on these hills that the earliest stirrings of the National Park movement took place, with the demands for rights of access to the moors, culminating in the "Battle for Kinder" in the 1930s. This gave rise to the National Parks and Access to the Countryside Act of 1949. There is a walk in the book which focuses on Hayfield, the meeting place of the campaigners prior to their demonstrations.

The National Park attracts around 22 million visitors each year. The vast majority simply make a day visit, for walking, sightseeing or other recreational activity. Similarly, the overwhelming majority come by car rather than public transport and this brings in its wake problems of traffic congestion and parking. Contending with such numbers is no easy task and in the Hope Valley and Derwent Dams, schemes have been adopted to avoid the traffic jams that make life unpleasant for all. The same argument, however, also applies to footpaths, for heavy usage like this can cause maintenance problems if not properly managed. It is important for walkers to support the conservation and maintenance work of the various footpath authorities. For the most part, the authors have chosen less-well-used paths but in some places it has been necessary to include very popular sections.

A brief history

The Peak District probably retains more evidence of its past than most other regions of England. It has not been buried in a welter of rebuilding and "improvement". The isolated rugged landscape and harsh, upland climate, have served to retain ample evidence of the earliest inhabitants and their successors in a quite remarkable way.

Like most upland areas of northern Britain, the Peak District enjoys a "moist" climate – a typical Derbyshire understatement. The dark peat bogs on Kinder, Bleaklow and Howden Moors are legendary. The rivers are fast flowing and soon attracted the attention of 18th-century industrialist.

Few Peakland valleys are wholly lacking evidence of water-powered mills or factories. Similarly, few have escaped the 19th- and 20th-century municipal reservoir. Opinion is divided on the landscape impact of these sheets of water, but it would be a purist of the deepest dye who would deny that the view over Ladybower reservoir is exceptionally attractive, especially with the backdrop of hills, and when the trees are in their autumnal splendour.

Ladybower is one of the three reservoirs that make up the Derwent Dams complex. The earlier two, Derwent and Howden are massive stone structures and are very impressive, especially when overflowing. These were used for training the "Dambuster" Squadron during the Second World War. Ladybower on the other hand is an earth-covered dam, recently raised to comply with new safety legislation. Ladybower is the Peak's biggest single sheet of water. It cradles two drowned villages of Derwent and Ashopton. In the woodlands around the reservoirs lie the remains of farms, abandoned when their land was acquired by the water committees. The authors have included two rambles, Ashopton and Ladybower, to introduce you to this part of the Dark Peak.

The abandonment of upland farms is nothing new however. As agricultural demand and supply has changed over the centuries so farming has ebbed and flowed up and down the hillsides. There is, once again, a fear of an exodus from the hill farms because of changing regulations and subsidy regimes emanating from the European Union. This is one of the major changes witnessed by the authors in the preparation of this second edition; many farms have now become places to live in rather than as a base to work the land.

There is abundant evidence of early settlement on the high gritstone moorlands, dating back thousands of years before the Roman conquest. Village sites, field systems, fortresses, burial places; all are there on areas like Big Moor, east of Baslow. Moors that are now inhospitable

Milestone below the Cat and Fiddle

heather and bracken-clad peat were once tree clad and farmed. The earliest known trackways date from these pre-Roman times and some are still in use today. The Roman occupation left less impression on the Dark Peak than on the White Peak, but some of the Roman roads survive. One such route came from the fort at Glossop (Melandra), over the flanks of Kinder and Win Hill to Brough (Navio) and thence southwards to Derby. Another came up from Leek, via Buxton (Aquae Arnemetiae) to Brough and thence to Rotherham. Yet another ran from Buxton to Glossop via Hayfield and from Buxton skirting the Goyt valley en route to Manchester. Remains of all these exist and are in use by the walker and, in certain parts, by motor traffic.

As a measure of the change that has taken place since the legions left, it is worth noting that the Roman road across the Snake Pass has been covered by almost 2 metres (6 feet) of peat, which has accumulated in the intervening 1600 years. The first retreat from the uplands was a combination of climatic and technological change. The weather grew colder and wetter and technologically the equipment became available to clear the denser woods and to plough the heavier soils of the valleys.

Saxon occupation came late to the Peak District. The evidence is there in the survival of Celtic place names like Dinas, Derwent and Eccles. This last name is evidence of a survival of Celtic Christianity. Even the name of the Peak's highest hill, Kinder Scout, is thought by some to derive from the Celtic "Cwm Dwr Scwd", meaning "the valley of the waterfall". This seems an odd name for a hill, until you remember that Kinder's best-known feature is The Downfall.

Later conquerors, such as the Danes and the Normans, laid a veneer on the ancient bones of Peakland, adding their castles and settlements and their own place names. The "booths" in Edale and the numerous hills called "Low" spring to mind. Norman-French names include words like "Roaches", meaning "rocks" and "Chapel en le Frith", the "church in the forest".

In the Norman period, and for many centuries afterwards, huge tracts of the High Peak became royal hunting forests. Peak Forest was subject to the strictest of forest laws. The word 'forest' is something of a misnomer, for they were not true wooded forests, but wild and relatively unpopulated areas made even wilder by forced depopulation and dispersal of the inhabitants. Peak Forest was divided into three "wards": the high moors of Kinder and Bleaklow formed the Longdendale ward; the Hope and Edale valleys were the Hopedale ward; and the area between Buxton and Hayfield was known as the "Campagna". Boundaries of this Forest and its wards were marked and Edale Cross is believed to be one such marker.

Enforcement of the forest laws required staff and one such was the Woodreeve. This key official is remembered in the pub name in Hope, the Woodruffe Arms. As the centuries went by the history of the Forest is littered with attempts by farmers and others to encroach on the royal preserve, finally succeeding in the 17th century, though the Crown still holds large tracts of land in the former Forest, especially around Castleton.

Mention has been made of the enduring legacy of Christianity in the Peak. The Christian church established in Roman times seems to have endured the subsequent Saxon and Danish invasions. By the Middle Ages the church was a vitally important part of everyday life and was responsible for land management on a vast scale. The Middle Ages were known as the Age of Faith, and travel in the Dark Peak must have required a hefty slice of that commodity. Even as late as the 18th century, there are tales of guides being needed to cross the East Moors. The lonely wayside crosses such as Edale Cross, Hope Cross and Lady Cross were important markers in the wilderness, not superseded until the edict of 1709 required the placing of guide-stoops at main crossroads. These were the first real road signs, pointing the way to the nearest market town. Some of the crosses survive as do many of the guide-stoops and they still serve their original function, though now largely for the leisure traveller on foot.

As traffic on the Peak District roads and tracks increased as a result of increasing prosperity, so too did the temptation to "supplement ones income", by a crafty bit of highway robbery. Legends of local highway-men abound, particularly on the western fringes of the Peak between Buxton and Macclesfield, but there are some particularly macabre legends surrounding the old road from Darley Dale over to Chesterfield. The Peak District must have been a dangerous place for the salter making his way with his precious commodity from the Cheshire lowlands across to Yorkshire and north-east Derbyshire. No wonder there were inns built in the quietest of locations to afford refuge to these tradesmen. Fortunately, many have survived through to this day.

With the onset of the agrarian and industrial revolutions, the scene again was one of agricultural encroachment onto the moors. Enclosure and land improvement were the order of the day. Food was needed for the rapidly growing towns that fringed the Peak. With this came improvements in transport on a tremendous scale. The old packhorse and cart tracks were widened and straightened. Much of the pres-ent-day main-road network dates from the second half of the 18th century and the first quarter of the 19th. Consequently, many of the old routes, too steep for "modern" carriages and carts, either were extin-guished as roads or simply fell out of use. Much of this earlier network remains, now reverted to pleasant grassy tracks, trodden only by the occasional pedestrian.

As population expanded, so too did the demand for more moorland to be taken into farming. This process was aided by improved machin-ery and by changing agricultural practices, but also by a warming climate, recovering from the "Little Ice Age" of the 18th century. Further changes to agricultural economics, particularly the cheaper imports of food made possible by improved shipping and the opening up of the American prairies, led to a retrenchment from the hills or their conversion to vast sheep walks. Other moors became almost as exclu-sive as they had been in the days of the royal forest, with attempts by some landowners to deny access on to the moors and even stop off ancient rights of way in the interests of sheep farming and the breeding and shooting of game birds.

This attitude, coupled with the understandable desire of town dwellers to leave the "dark satanic mills" behind on their few days off, led to the pressure for a "right to roam" open moorlands. The National Park movement in this country was largely fuelled by this debate. High profile events like the mass trespasses and the "Battle" for Kinder are still recalled.

Peak & Northern footpath sign

The struggle for a right of access went on through most of the 20th century and has only recently been enshrined in law as part of the Countryside and Rights of Way Act. Walkers using this book will come across both access land, where they can wander at will and moorland where, at present, the only access is by using a public right of way crossing it. This, however, will change in some areas as a result of legislation affecting areas categorised as 'mountain, moorland, heath and downland'.

A tale of pubs and public transport

One of the great bonuses of enjoying any walk is the ability to adjourn to a local hostelry for a good pint of ale. Whether this is at the end of the day or as a respite at lunchtime matters not. Peak District inns have for centuries welcomed the traveller on foot though now the person arriving at the country pub on foot is most likely to be a recreational walker rather than a farmer, miner or quarryman. Most country pubs are now geared to a leisure clientele, but despite this shift the tradition of hospitality and serving good ale, remains. Here we take our hats off to the Campaign for Real Ale (CAMRA), champions of the cause of good beer and the retention of the character of local pubs. CAMRA has done far more for the discerning drinker than most big breweries would care to admit. If you would like to join this consumer organisation campaigning for quality beer then have a look at their website: www.camra.org.uk. You will find that there are several local branches which cover the Peak District.

The snag for the rambler who loves real ale is of course that drinking and driving, when mixed, are a lethal cocktail. All the rambles in this book feature at least one pub, so those people who find it impossible to pass a pub without sampling a tipple should let someone else do the driving. How about using a professional? Use the local bus or train. This helps keep congestion down and puts money into a vital local facility.

Using the local bus

All of the walks in this book are accessible by public transport. In fact, the authors used buses and trains to survey the walks again. We give details of the available bus and train services for each walk, but you are strongly advised to purchase a copy of Derbyshire County Council's excellent Peak District timetable – it has to be one of the most comprehensive available in the country. Best to check before you travel, so call the Traveline number for up to the minute details of bus timings. The number is 0870 608 2608. For trains contact National Rail Enquiries on 08457 48 49 50. Derbyshire County Council's public transport website has details of all services and an interactive journey planner facility. The address is www.derbybus.net.

There are various ticket offers that make travelling by bus and/or train an attractive financial proposition. Details are contained in the Peak District timetable or from the website. One of the best is the Wayfarer ticket, which comes in two forms, one covering the whole of Derbyshire (Derbyshire Wayfarer) and the other covering Greater Manchester and most of the National Park. Worth buying for a good ride round the area, let alone for accessing these walks. These tickets are available at railway and bus stations, some tourist information offices and post offices. The Derbyshire Wayfarer is also available from the

driver on some bus companies. Some of the walks are best accessed
from Sheffield and the South Yorkshire Passenger Transport Executive
have a Traveline on 01709 515151 available everyday. On the Manchester side of the Peak District, Greater Manchester Passenger Transport
Executive provides an information line which can be contacted on 0161
228 7811

About this book

This book is a sister publication to "Pub Walks in the White Peak".
Encouraged by the success of this first volume, the authors proceeded
to sample the delights (both pedestrian and pub) of the Dark Peak.
Hence this book. The Dark Peak can be defined as the northern part of
the National Park, plus its western and eastern fringes. Companion
books in this series cover North Staffordshire, Cheshire and the South
Pennines, so we have been careful to avoid duplication.

We take the walker mainly to the gritstone areas of the Peak, the high
northern moors and the enchanting hills fringing the inner limestone
plateau. Some walks venture outside the National Park into the shale
valleys that spill down to the surrounding towns and cities. The walks
range from 3 miles to 11 miles. A few are easy but most include some
climbs and thus require a little effort and in some cases real stamina. At
the beginning of each route, the authors include the nature of the walk.

For some, the name "Dark Peak" sounds uninviting. It is a harsher
environment than the White Peak, but the compensations are manifold;
the wildness, the dramatic scenery, the interplay of rocks, heather and
cascading water. In the words of the famous Ewan McColl song;

I go where I will, over valley and hill, and I lie where the bracken is
deep.
I belong to the mountains, to those dear crystal fountains and the
rocks that are rugged and steep.
I have seen the white hare in the heather, and the curlew fly high
overhead.
And sooner than part from the mountains, I think I would rather be
dead.

Don your boots now, and make for the Peak's highest hills.

Walk 1. Ashopton

The Route: Heatherdene, Ashopton, Ladybower Tor, Whinstone Lee Tor, Hurkling Stones, Highshaw Clough, Moscar House, Ladybower Inn, Heatherdene. (Optional extension to Wheel Stones, White Tor and the Salt Cellar)

Distance: 4 miles. Allow 2½ hours exclusive of stops. The optional extension lengthens the walk by 2 miles and a further hour.

Start: Heatherdene car park (Grid reference 203 860)

Map: OS Explorer OL 1, The Peak District, Dark Peak Area.

How to get there:

By bus – *Daily service, buses 273/274 from Sheffield, alight at the entrance to Heatherdene car park. Seasonal services, buses 373,473 and 673 operate from Glossop and Manchester.*

By car – *From the Sheffield or Manchester directions, follow the A57 to its junction with the A6013, then follow this road for about ½ mile to Heatherdene car park (signed on the left). From the south, make your way into the Hope Valley and join the A6013 at the Marquis of Granby traffic lights. Go through Bamford village and past Ladybower dam to Heatherdene car park.*

By train – *Daily service from Manchester and Sheffield to Bamford station, but this adds another 3 miles to the walk.*

The Pub

The Ladybower Inn near Bamford (tel: 01433 651241) was originally located in the old hamlet at Ashopton which was flooded by the Ladybower dam. Now it stands well above the water level by the A57 road with excellent views across the waters to Win Hill. The inn features material displayed around the pub to reflect the history of the area, the old village and the Dambusters Squadron (617). The Dambusters practised their manoeuvres over the Derwent and Howden dams before the famous raid on the Ruhr dams during the Second World War.

The inn comprises one main lounge bar and there is also outside seating which is popular in summer. The pub is open from 11am every

The Ladybower Inn

day until closing time. It serves on hand-pull Barnsley Bitter, Marston's Pedigree and Green King's Ruddles County. Food is served from 12 noon-2.30pm and from 5-9.30pm Mondays to Saturdays and from 12 noon until 9.30pm on Sundays. Wherever possible the food is sourced from the local farming community. Families are welcome and overnight accommodation is available – see www.ladybower-inn.co.uk.

The Walk

The walk is moderately strenuous in that there are a few steep climbs to tackle en route but on most sections it is easy. From Heatherdene car park go down the main entrance road to the A6013, cross the road and turn right. Follow the footpath-cum-cycleway alongside Ladybower reservoir, with fine views across the water to Ashopton viaduct and Crook Hill. Cross Ladybower viaduct and at the traffic lights turn left, now following the A57. Ashopton village lay just below you, straggled along the old route of the A57. Like its sister village of Derwent, Ashopton was flooded when Ladybower reservoir was created. Unlike Derwent, its remains never resurfaced, so deeply are they drowned. Just before you reach Ashopton viaduct, cross the road and go up the lane on

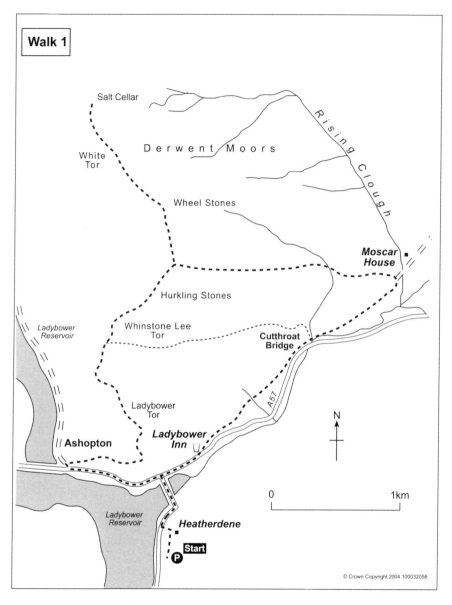

Walk 1

Salt Cellar

Rising Clough

White Tor

D e r w e n t M o o r s

Wheel Stones

Moscar House

Hurkling Stones

Ladybower Reservoir

Whinstone Lee Tor

Cutthroat Bridge

A57

Ladybower Tor

N

Ashopton

Ladybower Inn

0   1km

Ladybower Reservoir

Heatherdene

Start

P

© Crown Copyright 2004 100032058

the opposite side. After less than 100 metres, go sharp right, up another lane. This was the old, pre-turnpike route from Sheffield to Glossop. It climbs steadily away from the successor road.

Ladybower viaduct

Beyond the group of buildings marked on the map as Ashopton, the lane degenerates into a track, soon passing Ding Bank Farm. Continue up the track, pass through a gate onto the steeply sloping hillside and you are soon treated to a birds-eye view of Ladybower viaduct.

Continue along the track, with the wall to your right, until you reach the point where the track begins to descend slightly. At the junction pylon a narrow path diverges left, up the hill and this is your route. Climb steeply up Ladybower Tor, until, at a solitary thorn bush you enter a series of overgrown hollow-ways. A distinct path continues upwards, soon emerging on the top of Lead Hill, where there is a magnificent view of the Derwent valley, north and south. The path now makes its way along the edge, with the high moorlands of the Dark Peak dominating the western horizon and the waters of Ladybower reservoir adding a dash of colour to the scene.

Whinstone Lee Tor

Stroll along the edge path, soon crossing the route from Cutthroat Bridge. If limbs are tired or the weather has turned inclement this route to the right leads unerringly to the old road again and saves retracing your steps. The walk goes straight ahead at this point, following the obvious path along the edge, making for Whinstone Lee Tor. When you top this rise, Derwent Edge stretches ahead of you, with the various rock formations clearly in view. Make your way along the edge, soon passing the Hurkling Stones and thus reach another cross "roads" with a line of shooting butts off to the right. This is the turning point of the main walk and if you are not going to do the extension, you should turn right here, on the path signed to Moscar. However, the Wheel Stones can be seen only 500m away and look inviting for a crafty scramble, so press on, but remember this spot when you return.

The Wheel Stones are well worth a stop and a scramble. Getting onto the highest rocks is easy enough. Getting off is a different matter. You have been warned. The path runs just to the left of the outcrop, with grand views on all sides. The next pile of rocks is White Tor and this is closely followed by another jumble, shown on the map as the Salt Cellar. This is not the name of the group of rocks, but is a very apt description of one particular rock, shaped very much like an old-fashioned salt cellar. It is easily missed as it lies on the north-western side of the pile of rocks, overlooking Derwent reservoir. Only its top can be seen from the path, but if you find that you have reached a wall on your left, you have passed the Salt Cellar.

Derwent Edge stretches away before you, and there is a strong temptation to carry on, but it is time to turn round and retrace your steps, past White Tor, and the Wheel Stones to the Moscar-Derwent signpost. Here turn left. The path veers away to the right of the shooting butts and is obvious throughout. There are few markers on this moor, but there is one obvious standing stone and soon you reach another line of shooting butts, very close to the path. The path, now wide enough to accommodate a Land Rover, dips to cross Highshaw Clough Brook. You climb away from the brook and continue over the moor to the intake wall around Moscar House Farm. Stanage Edge can be seen to the right. Go ahead through the gate and follow the wall down, under the electricity line, bearing right to the stile by the gates.

Guide Stone

Go over the stile, or through the adjacent gate, which should be signed, but the signpost was broken when the walk was reconnoitred. You are now back onto the old Sheffield-Glossop road again. Follow the old road across the field to a stile, beside which there is a fine example of a guide stone. The writing is visible on three faces, but is difficult to decipher. Only the Sheffield road inscription is really clear. The three inscriptions read; SHEFFIELD ROAD 7M EP (EP is presumably the initials of the surveyor), -STO –ROAD 11, —-D –OAD 4M. Any offers as to the derivation of the other two would be very welcome.

Go over the stile, onto open moorland. Follow the old road over the moor, with the new road down in the clough on your left. Ladybower Brook and Cutthroat Bridge can be seen below as the old road keeps company with the power lines to Highshaw Clough. At Highshaw Clough the map shows the line of the old road as a right of way, but the bridge is long gone, presumably when the turnpike was constructed in 1818. The abutments still exist on either side and it must have been a substantial bridge in its day. This is the original Cutthroat Bridge, which gained its macabre name from an incident in 1635. A man was found in Eashaw (Highshaw) Clough with a "wound in his throat", and was carried down to Ladybower House where he died.

Once over the stream, continue along the old road, with good views across to Bamford and Hordron Edges. You soon descend to a gate by a ford and enter the Derbyshire Wildlife Trust's Ladybower Wood Nature

Reserve. The view left is now obscured by oak woodland, but this is of interest in its own right, being a remnant of the once extensive tree cover that carpeted these moors. A further gentle stroll sees the track beginning to descend and soon you reach a gate by another DWT sign. The old road continues to the right, but you go through the gate and down to the pub, now seen below.

Telford's Turnpike

You emerge on Telford's 1818 turnpike road, right by the Ladybower Inn, which certainly is an inducement to pause and partake of refreshment as your walk is nearly finished. There are buses back to Sheffield from the inn.

On leaving the pub, cross the road with care and go along the verge toward the viaduct, seen ahead and to the left. On your left as you look down into this short arm of the reservoir, you can see the old bridge and the remains of the Bamford road, which is frequently under water.

At the traffic lights, turn left across the viaduct. There is no footway beyond the viaduct so you ought to cross over. If you are heading for Heatherdene car park you will have to cross the road again, so it is probably safer to stay on this side and make your way along the verge to the Fishery Office. From here there is a footway back to Heatherdene.

Walk 2. Baslow

The Route: Baslow Nether End, Chatsworth Park, Queen Mary's Bower, Edensor, Pilsley, Rymas Brook, Baslow Old Bridge.

Distance: 9km (6 miles). Allow 3 hours exclusive of stops.

Start: Baslow car park (pay and display). (Grid reference 258 721)

Map: OS Explorer OL 24 – The Peak District, White Peak Area.

How to get there:

By bus – *There are daily bus services from Bakewell (170, 240 and X18), Buxton (66 and X18), Chesterfield (TM Travel X67, Hulleys 170), Manchester (X67), Matlock (214, 240 and X18), Stockport (X67) and Stoke on Trent to Baslow (X18).*

By car – *From Chesterfield follow the A619 to Baslow. From Sheffield follow the A621 to Baslow.*
From Buxton follow the A6 then the A6020 from Ashford to join the A619 just east of Bakewell for Baslow.
From Manchester follow the A6 to Barmoor Clough then the A623 to Baslow.

The Pub

The Devonshire Arms at Pilsley [tel: 01246 583258] is a traditional country pub located conveniently close to the Chatsworth House farm shop in the village of Pilsley. The pub is also part of the Chatsworth estate. The pub is not only a convivial local for the residents of the village but also welcomes walkers and other visitors. Many people walk the recognised paths across the estate and return to the pub afterwards to take refreshment.

The pub sells a changing range of cask ales. It is open from 11.30am (11am on Saturdays) until 3pm on Mondays to Saturdays, then from early evening onwards, and it is open normal hours on Sundays. Home-cooked food is served from 12 noon until 2pm daily and there is a carvery available on Thursday, Friday and Saturday evenings. There is overnight accommodation available. Families are welcome and one room is made available especially for family groups.

The Walk

Fairly easy walking through delightful parkland is the order of the day. From Baslow Nether End car park and bus stops, go past the little shop, along the lane and over the Barbrook Bridge. This bridge originally carried the main Chesterfield road into Baslow, before it was diverted to avoid Chatsworth parkland. Once over the bridge, turn right and follow a good path towards Chatsworth Park.

Another path trails in from the right and here you bear left, soon passing through a revolving "stile" into open parkland. There follows a mile of easy and delightful walking on paths and estate roads. The route keeps close to the River Derwent, except where the walled gardens, cricket pitch and campsite intervene. To the left the land rises steeply to the Hunting Tower. Ahead, at a lower level, the Palace of the Peak, Chatsworth House, soon comes into view.

Chatsworth House and Park

Chatsworth House and Park are among the Peak District's greatest tourist attractions. They can generate traffic jams in the height of summer and on days when there are major events, e.g. the horse trials, the grounds can be closed except on payment of an entrance fee. Check your dates.

The house and gardens you see today were laid out between 1687 and 1707 on behalf of William Cavendish, the First Duke of Devonshire. His successors have lived here ever since and have allowed public access to both the Park and the House. The House and Gardens are well worth a visit, but not on this walk, unless you have allowed all day. The path keeps close to the river until the ruins of Queen Mary's Bower are reached. This structure is a reminder of the tragic Mary, Queen of Scots, who was held prisoner at the earlier Chatsworth House at various times between 1570 and 1581. The Bower is a raised, moated structure, approached by a single flight of steps, delightful, but an effective prison.

Beyond the Bower, go right and cross the bridge. This bridge was part of the great rebuilding in the last part of the 17th century. Before that, an earlier bridge carried the Bakewell to Chesterfield road over the Derwent. The making of the parkland in the 1690s caused the closure of this road.

Just beyond the bridge, bear right, leaving the road and heading along a broad path towards the village of Edensor (pronounced 'Enser').

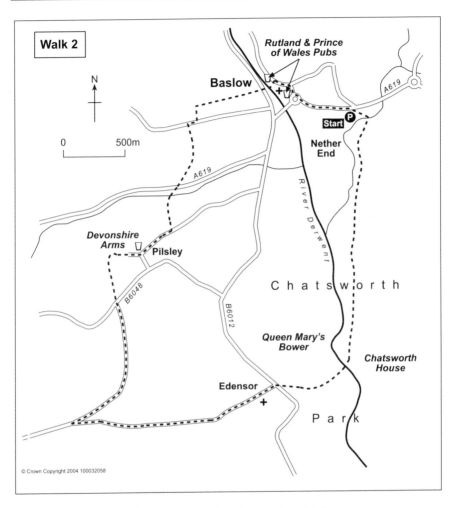

This path was the alignment of the old road, which soon appears as a terrace as the path rises up the bank and the village comes into view.

Edensor

Cross the main road with care and enter the village. The settlement is owned by Chatsworth estates and was built in the mid-19th century, allegedly to replace the old village, the houses of which spoiled the Duke's view! New Edensor is most unusual in design and layout. No two houses are the same. It is entirely surrounded by a wall and fence to prevent cattle getting in. The central feature is the impressive church,

Overlooking the Chatsworth Estate

which stands raised up above the rest of the village. It dates from the 1860s and is to a design by Gilbert Scott. It was completed in 1870. In the churchyard is the grave of the sister of the late President J.F. Kennedy. She was married to the Marquis of Hartington, eldest son of the 6th Duke.

Go through the village keeping the church to your left. The village street soon narrows to a lane, which then deteriorates still further to become a rough track. This was once the main Chesterfield to Bakewell road mentioned earlier. After about a mile of easy though uphill walking, you join another road.

Pilsley

At the road junction, turn right, noting on your right the guide stone. This is dated 1709 and has the three towns of Bakewell, Chesterfield and Sheffield incised upon it. You now follow the "Sheffield" road. There is a very good view from here – up the Derwent valley towards Fox House, Higger Tor, Baslow and Curbar Edges – to the west to Hassop Common, Longstone Edge and Fin Cop, with even a glimpse of the higher hills near Mam Tor and Rushop.

Stroll down the road, passing Paddock's Plantation on your right and soon you reach a T-junction (buses to Baslow and Bakewell from here in extremis.) Cross the main road and go over a stile and into a field. The exit is another stile straight ahead, leading into a green lane on the same alignment as the road you have just walked down. At one time this was a continuation of the same lane. The green lane bends right. Ignore the branch leading off left, down into the valley of the Rymas Brook, and continue straight on into Pilsley, noting the 30mph restriction signs as you enter the village. On this basis you were allowed to drive at 60mph on the green lane.

Pilsley is another Chatsworth estate village and boasts a church, shop, post office and pub, not surprisingly called the Devonshire Arms. A brief call for a bite to eat and a thirst quencher may be called for.

Local Wells

On leaving the pub continue down the main street, soon leaving the village behind. In the garden of the last house is an old grindstone and opposite is a white gate, which protects a well. This is a reminder that, not so long ago, most Peak District villages relied heavily on local wells and springs for their water supply.

Baslow Edge and the other eastern edges are in view as you walk down the road. When you reach the barn, go left, over an unsigned stile, by a sycamore tree. Once in the field, the path keeps to the left of the wall and descends gently towards the valley of the Rymas Brook. Where the gradient steepens, look out for a stile and gate in the wall on your right and go over and through them.

The path now slants steeply down across the field, with Baslow Edge prominently in view ahead. Note on the opposite side of the Rymas Brook an electricity pole in the field. This will be a useful marker in a few minutes time. Follow the well-blazed path down to a well-hidden bridge and stile. This leads out onto the main A619 road.

Cross the road with care and go through the stile opposite. Head up the field to the electricity pole spotted earlier and cross the field to the left of a shallow depression to reach a gate at the wall corner. Do not go through the gate but follow the path round the field boundary to a stile. This gives out onto a minor road, which was once the main route west out of Baslow.

Baslow

Go right here, towards Baslow, which can be seen ahead. If time presses, you can carry on down the lane into the village, but the route of the walk goes left at the next signed footpath. The path crosses the field to a prominent upright stone in the wall. Here, imperceptibly there is a crossing of paths and here you turn right. Follow the wall straight ahead, descending through a series of fields, down a paved way between houses, to emerge on the road, almost opposite the old bridge over the Derwent.

Cross the fine medieval bridge, restored in the 17th century. On the far side is a curious little stone shelter, built into the parapet. It has variously been described as a toll keeper's hut or a guard post. The latter seems to be the more likely.

From the bridge, follow the main road round past the church. Note the clock on the church tower. Instead of the usual numerals, it has the word VICTORIA and the date 1897 to commemorate Victoria's diamond jubilee. This was the idea of a local resident, Dr Wrench, who 30 years earlier had organised the erection of the Wellington Monument on Baslow Edge. Unfortunately for timekeeping, the 1, 8, 9 and 7 on the clock face are not coincident with the hours 1, 8, 9 or 7. Could be useful though, if there is any dispute about pub opening hours. Inside the church, one of the artefacts is a dog whip, with which the churchwarden would drive out any stray dogs (or possibly drunken vagrants).

Just beyond the church is a pub, the Prince of Wales. From here it is but a short step along the main road, past the roundabout and the Cavendish Hotel to reach the main bus stops at Baslow (Nether End) where there are other hostelries and a café that welcome walkers.

Walk 3. Bollington

The Route: Middlewood Way, Kerridge old tramway, Kerridge Ridge, Waulkmill, Ingersley Vale, Sowcar

Distance: 4 miles. Allow 2 hours exclusive of stops.

Start: Car park and information centre on Adlington Road, Bollington (Grid reference 932781)

Map: OS Explorer OL 24 – The Peak District, White Peak Area.

How to get there:

By bus – *Daily service (buses 10, 11, 12, 391/2) from Macclesfield and Stockport. Ask for the Dog and Partridge public house. The bus stops about 150 metres beforehand.*

By car – *From Macclesfield follow the B5090 through to Bollington. It is signed from the main Silk Road. Turn left after the viaduct before the Dog and Partridge public house.*

The Pub

The Poachers Inn (tel: 01625 572086) is situated at the end of a group of terraced houses. It is a welcoming hostelry, which offers Timothy Taylor's Landlord, and an ever-changing range of guest beers. The landlord and landlady have developed a reputation for excellent beer and fine food and thanks to their good work the pub has been featured in the CAMRA Good Beer Guide in recent years.

Whilst the pub has one bar situated mid-way into the pub, there remain a number of different drinking corners, which make it feel cosy; there's always reading material, local CAMRA publications and the like, for those who want a quiet read while they relax. At the end of the bar there is a superb non-smoking restaurant and access to a rear garden, which is very popular. Being so close to the Gritstone Trail, and near to paths which lead up to that well known landmark folly, White Nancy on Kerridge Ridge, the pub really is ideally situated for walkers.

The Poachers Inn is open from 12-2pm on Tuesdays to Saturdays and again from 5.30pm in the evening, but from 7pm on Saturdays, Sundays 12-2.30pm and from 7pm. Food is served at lunch and evening but not on Mondays. Check the website for details on www.thepoachersinnbollington.co.uk.

The Walk

In terms of effort required the walk is best divided into two. The first part includes steep climbs and is moderately strenuous. The second half is far gentler stuff. From the car park on Adlington Road, follow the steps, located at the rear of car park and children's play area, up to the Middlewood Way. Go left to walk across the impressive structure, once part of the railway from Macclesfield to Marple Rose Hill. It is much loved by the residents of Bollington who campaigned some years ago for its restoration against a threat of demolition. Thankfully they won the day. Continue ahead on the trail (which is also used by cyclists) for a short distance to Grimshaw Lane, a pleasant enough walk marred only by a small number of uncaring dog walkers.

At Grimshaw Lane, turn left to walk up to the canal overbridge. Just before, cross over the road and walk up steps set in the retaining wall which give out onto the towpath of the Macclesfield Canal, built in the 1830s for the Duke of Bridgewater, and more or less following a 500 foot contour line across the east of Cheshire. On the right is the Adelphi Mill, which in the 1850s was a formidable steam powered cotton mill. It now comprises offices and workshops mainly.

Leave the towpath at the next bridge, number 28, by way of a fine set of stone steps. Go left over the bridge and proceed along the track ahead, ignoring the one that forks to the left. Pass Bobbin Cottage, a reminder that there was at one time a Bobbin works here in the 19th century. Continue to a small belt of trees. Just before, go right through the kissing gate to enter a field. Walk ahead to a footbridge and gate, then ahead again to join an old track. Look to the right and the left. You will see that this track, which was a tramway, runs from a wharf up the hillside to Kerridge Ridge and it is as straight as can be.

The Old Tram Road

Go left to follow the old Kerridge tramway up the incline to Kerridge. This little engineering masterpiece was built in the 1830s to transport stone from the Kerridge quarries to the canal. Cross Clarke Lane and continue ahead as the incline steepens, passing through the gateway to Endon House. Proceed up the drive to Endon Cottage where the last stretch of the tramway, believe it or not, used to rise steeply beneath the road bridge above. The place looks so tranquil now but this would have been the scene of intense industrial activity one hundred and fifty years ago. The dust must have been overpowering, and certainly bad for the

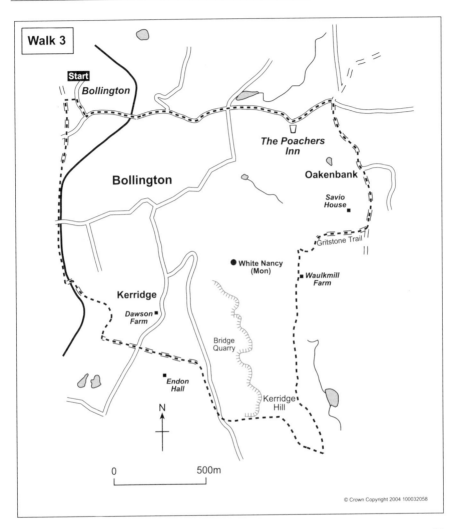

health of the tramway workers. The much-prized Kerridge Stone is still quarried but on a much smaller scale than hitherto.

Your way is to turn right before Endon Cottage, up the drive, to leave the houses behind and to rise up to a road. Cross over and walk ahead towards the entrance to Endon Quarry. Before the gate, turn right up a narrow path, as signposted, then follow it as it bends left and climbs up the hillside by cottages. Be careful as the workings below are some way down and hence the path is potentially dangerous.

Kerridge Ridge

Cross a stile about half way up and then proceed to cross two stiles at the top of Kerridge Ridge. The views across to Rainow and the Western Peakland are magnificent. Tempting as it might be, do not turn left or right to walk along the ridge. Keep ahead instead on a wide green path, which plummets down the hillside between hawthorns. Be vigilant here, as within 10 metres, your way is the lower, less distinct path heading downwards in the direction of Rainow.

It is hard to believe that this side of the ridge has also been the subject of extractive mining, mainly for coal and that the valley below was the site of several water-powered textile mills. Head for the solitary hawthorn mid-field and, on nearing this point, you will see a cross-path. The River Dean can be seen below this and beyond is Hough Hole House where there is a Victorian allegorical garden, known as Mellors Garden, based on the Pilgrims Progress.

Turn left at the hawthorn, and walk to the next field boundary, where a stone step-stile is crossed. The path rises left to skirt a tree belt, sheltering a house to the right. Go through a gate and follow the path across the next field, with stone slabs or 'causeys' evident on the ground. Pass through the stone gateway and take the right fork, which leads to a stile, and a wood owned by The Woodland Trust. The path descends through the wood to a wooden gate. Go through it and pass by a cottage to a road. The cascade of water to the right is where the Dean was dammed (rather than damned as we wrote in the last edition) to produce a head of water for the mills in the valley.

Ingersley Vale

Continue ahead as the road drops down towards the old mill buildings in Ingersley Vale. Beforehand, look for a path off to the right; it is part of the Gritstone Trail. Cross the stile, go over the bridge and then bear left to climb up the hillside to a gap-stile and up steps to another stile. There is a delightful little dell to the left and then the grounds of Savio House; please note that these grounds are private. Thus ignore the first ladder stile on the left as you proceed up the field. Walk on to a wooden stile but as soon as this is crossed go left to cross a stone step-stile.

The path proceeds to cross a stile by a dwelling and then it keeps company with a wall on the left as it descends a number of steps to a bridge and then there is a slight ascent to the road. This is Oakenbank Lane. Follow it ahead to a crossroads at Blaze Hill. Here, you turn left and drop down to the Poachers Inn. After suitable refreshment, continue to walk along the road to the junction with the main road. This is the terminus for buses from Macclesfield and The Cotton Tree pub is a possible port of call. Those making their way back to Adlington Road should follow the main road through the town to the Dog and Partridge public house, where you turn right.

Walk 4. Bradwell

The Route: Bradwell, Grey Ditch, Botham's Farm, Rebellion Knoll, Robin Hood's Cross, Bradwell Edge, Bradwell.

Distance: 3 miles. Allow 2 hours exclusive of stops.

Start: Centre of Bradwell (Grid reference 174811). Limited on-street parking in the village.

Map: OS Explorer OL 1 – The Peak District, Dark Peak Area.

How to get there:

By bus – *There are daily services to Bradwell from Sheffield (bus 272) and Bakewell (bus 173) and summer seasonal services from other parts of the Peak District.*

By car – *From Sheffield use the A625 to Fox House, then the A6187 to the Travellers Rest, then the B6049 into Bradwell.*
From the west, pick up the A623 at Barmoor Clough and follow it to Anchor crossroads (Tideswell) then left onto the B6049 into Bradwell.

The Pub

There are three pubs in Bradwell, The New Bath Hotel, The Shoulder of Mutton and Ye Old Bowling Green (tel: 01433 620450). It is the latter that we recommend on this occasion. It is tucked away at the back of the village in Smalldale but well worth the extra 5-10 minutes walk. Ye Old Bowling Green is set back from the lane, known as Smalldale, overlooking the village. It is a very attractive historic inn dating from the 16th century made more attractive with climbing roses and hanging baskets adorning the original bay windows

The front entrance leads to several rooms served by a central bar and there are exposed original beams in places. The landlord has actually been able to recover several old parchments dating from previous centuries about the tenure of employment of staff. There is a restaurant in the old sitting room and garden room elevated to the rear of the pub, and a low bar, which serves a small room with fire to the left and a pool room to the right.

The pub is open at lunchtimes and evenings in the week and all day at weekends. It serves a range of beers including Draught Bass, Stones bitter, Timothy Taylor's Landlord and very often a guest ale. Food is served at these times. Families are welcome but children are to be accompanied by adults away from the bar. Dogs are not allowed. Ye Old Bowling Green has accommodation available – see www.yeoldbowling-greeninn.co.uk.

The Walk

This is easy walking in the Hope Valley. It is a good walk for limbering up to some of the more exacting rambles in the book. Bradwell lies on the Roman Road known as Batham Gate, which ran from Buxton to Templeborough (Rotherham). There was a fort at Brough and legend reckons that the inhabitants of Bradwell are descendants of the folk who worked the lead mines for the Romans and later for the new Saxon and Norman overlords. Bradwell still has the feel of being a working village rather than being taken over by tourists and commuters. A cabinet maker, builder's merchant and ice cream manufacturer have all survived and there is a busy atmosphere to the village, reminiscent of its mining heyday. Bradwell was once well known for the production of hard hats for miners, though not the sort of hard hat one finds nowadays used on construction sites or in mines. The Bradwell hats were known as "Bradda Beavers" and locals still sometimes refer to Bradwell as "Bradda".

Starting from the public toilets by the village green, turn right and walk to the main road. Go over the pelican crossing and down Soft Water Lane. The name refers to Bradwell Brook on the left. Follow the lane until you come to a stile on the right where you enter a small enclosure. Another squeezer stile leads out of this small field and a well-worn path then heads to the right of a barn. Keep on along this path, soon passing a recently rebuilt house to your left.

Grey Ditch

At the next straggly hedge the more obvious path goes straight on but life is never so straightforward. You bear right here on an indistinct path, heading up the field to a gate in the next hedge. The view begins to open out at this point, to the cement works and Losehill. Continue to climb gently across the next field, soon crossing a curious embankment. This is the Grey Ditch, reputedly of Romano-British vintage, but its purpose is unclear. A wooden stile lies just beyond the Ditch. Go

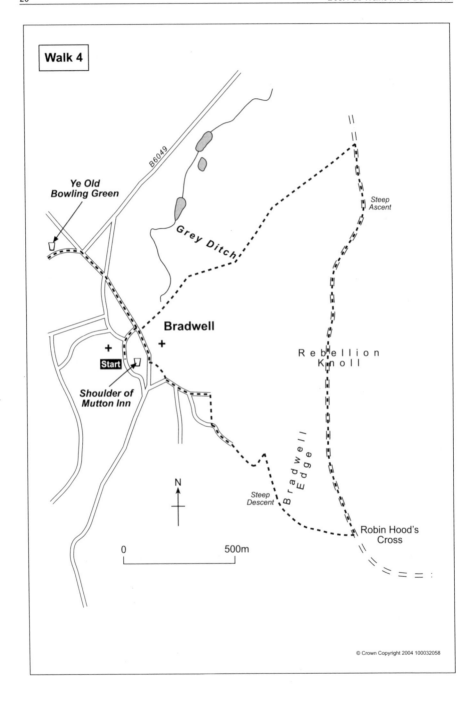

Walk 4

B6049

Ye Old
Bowling Green

Grey Ditch

Steep
Ascent

Bradwell

Start

*Shoulder of
Mutton Inn*

R e b e l l i o n
K n o l l

B
r
a
d
w
e
l
l

E
d
g
e

N

Steep
Descent

Steep
Descent

Robin Hood's
Cross

0   500m

© Crown Copyright 2004 100032058

through a wet patch and keep company with the hedge on your left, soon reaching a stile which gives out onto a farm track. Walk up the track towards Botham's Farm.

Just before the farm buildings, there is a stile on the right. Go over this and follow the edge of the field, above the buildings. The path dips to pass through a gate and then bears right, curving up the bank-side. The views towards Castleton are impressive, despite the cement works. Continue to contour the hillside, above the hawthorn scrub. The path forks and the more obvious path goes ahead to a gate, but this is not the right of way. Bear left, walk down through the scrub, to a stone gap-stile and thus onto a track.

Overdale

Once on the track, go right and climb quite steeply, with Overdale to your left and Shatton Moor beyond. Overdale is a Derbyshire Wildlife Trust nature reserve. The only decent views into it are from this track or Shatton Moor. The track eventually curves left and levels out. As you approach a gate, bear right and go over a stone step-stile. Go through the fields, with the wall to your left passing the point known as Robin Hood's Cross, another reference to that mythical character. You are quite likely to encounter hang glider enthusiasts on this section of the walk and you will be unlucky if you don't spot a glider from the Hucklow Edge gliding club site.

Suddenly you are confronted by a steep drop into Bradwell Dale, with an extensive view across the limestone plateau and northwards to the Losehill ridge and Kinder. Follow the well-blazed path down the hillside. It zigzags down to a wicket gate and stile before joining a track. Go down the track, passing a secluded house on your right. At the corner, just beyond the house, keep right, along a green lane that can be very overgrown. This soon joins another green lane, where you bear left and drop down into the village. The road twists a way between old cottages, eventually reaching the top of a flight of steps. Go down these to emerge on the main road, opposite the Shoulder of Mutton. Time now for a jar before catching the bus or returning to your car.

Walk 5. Calver Bridge

The Route: Calver Bridge, Townend Wood, Bubnell Farm, Oxpasture, Back Wood, Bramley Wood, Calver village, Calver Bridge.

Distance: 4½ miles. Allow 2½ hours exclusive of stops.

Start: Bridge Inn, Calver Bridge. Parking on old road by school. (Grid reference 248 744)

Map: OS Explorer OL 24 – The Peak District, White Peak Area.

How to get there:

By bus – *Daily services from Sheffield (buses 65 and 240), Chesterfield (buses 66, and X67), Manchester and Stockport (bus X67), Buxton (buses 65 or 66) and Bakewell (bus 240) to Calver Bridge.*

By car – *Calver Bridge lies on the A623 route across the Peak District.*

The Pub

The Bridge Inn at Calver Bridge (tel: 01433 630415) is a smashing old pub serving ales from the Kimberley brewery in Nottinghamshire. The same landlord and landlady were in charge when the pub was noted in the first edition of the book in 1992 and this long standing CAMRA Good Beer Guide entry remains as popular as ever with walkers and cyclists. There are a number of interesting features in this two-roomed pub including a large collection of antique fire fighting equipment. There is also an extensive garden by the River Derwent and next to the 18th-century bridge.

The pub serves Kimberley Best Bitter, Olde Trip and seasonal guest ales from the Hardy's and Hanson's brewery at Kimberley in Nottinghamshire. It is open from 11.30am until 3pm (3.30pm on Saturdays) and from 5.30pm on Mondays to Saturdays. On Sundays opening times are from 12 noon until 3.30pm and from 7pm until 10.30pm. Food is served daily at lunchtimes from 12 noon until 2.00pm and from 6.30pm until 8.30pm on Tuesdays to Saturdays. Families are welcome.

The Walk

This is a moderately easy walk. From the pub, go left, passing over the old bridge which spans the River Derwent. On the right, just beyond the

The Bridge Inn, Calver

bridge, is Calver Mill. This featured in the television series "Colditz", but has now been converted into luxury flats. Go left, under the new road and follow the riverside path, which now forms part of the Derwent Valley Heritage Way. The path crosses a footbridge over the sough tail. A sough, (pronounced 'suff'), is a tunnel for draining a mine. Calver Sough drained the lead mines to the west of Calver. The water sees daylight in the village and then runs as a stream to join the Derwent.

Beyond the sough the path soon reaches open fields and continues alongside the river. You soon enter a wood, where the path begins to draw away from the riverbank. On leaving the wood you enter a short section of walled lane. Look out for a stile in the wall as this is your route. The lane is probably a remnant of the former packhorse route, leading to the ancient river crossing of Stanton Ford. From the ford the packhorse way climbed over Curbar Gap and onto the moors heading for Chesterfield or Sheffield. Curbar Edge and the Gap can be seen as you look back.

Go through the stile and across the field to reach another stile to the left of a gate. Note the stone lined spring and water trough. Here you emerge onto a little used, and rather rough lane, where you turn left. Follow the lane, slightly uphill at first, towards Bubnell. At the 30mph signs, go right, up a narrow lane, passing Bubnell Grange on your left. Where the lane bears right to Bubnell farm, there is a signpost pointing left. This directs you alongside the Grange then through a gateway into a field. It is tempting to go straight ahead here as the path is not obvious, but this would be wrong. Instead, turn right, alongside the wall for a short way before veering slightly left to reach a gateway half way along the far wall. From the gateway you can see the Hunting Tower at the back of Chatsworth.

In the next field the path is again not obvious. The map suggests that you walk up the middle of the field, then turn left to reach the second of the two gateways in the left-hand wall. This gateway has a signpost and the evidence on the ground suggests that walkers simply cut the corner of the field, making a bee-line for the gate. Go through the gate and then pause to look back. The view up the valley is extensive, with the Eastern Edges particularly prominent.

Follow the wall on your left, to a stile to the left of a gate. Baslow is now in view to your left. Go over the stile and turn right, beside another wall. Continue up the field to a stile in the top right-hand corner, near a trough. Still going uphill beside a wall you reach another stile in the corner of the next field. Continue beside the wall to the corner, where a signpost directs you over the brow of the hill, in the general direction of a barn, seen some way ahead. As you top the rise, bear left across the field to a gateway in the far left-hand corner, and so reach a narrow lane.

Ancient Lane

This lane is ancient. It was once the main road from Chesterfield to Buxton and on to Manchester. It may even have Roman origins, as it lies in an excellent alignment between the fortresses of Chesterfield and Buxton and links known Romano-British settlements south of Monsal Dale. It was one of the early turnpikes, until superseded by the present main road through Stoney Middleton. Turn right on reaching the lane and follow it, soon topping the rise at the end of Toost Wood. Here the lane bends right and descends. Where it levels out, a signpost on the right directs you through a stile into a rough field.

Bear left to reach the edge of the wood. The exit from the field lies over a rickety stile into Bank Wood. The path is clear ahead, twisting its way through the wood, always keeping close to the wall on the right. When you emerge from the wood, Oxpasture Farm can be seen below to the left, while to the right lie the Eastern Edges. Across the valley to the

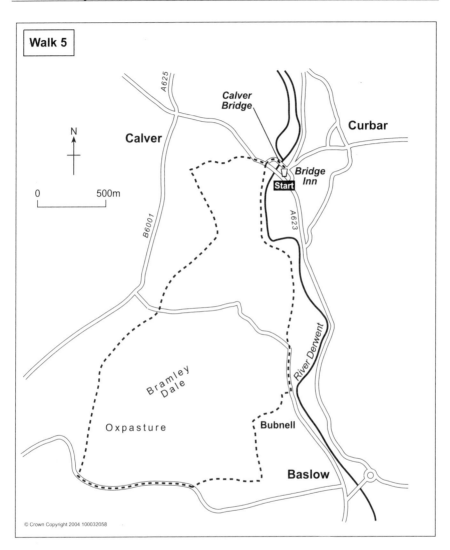

left is Hassop Common, an area extensively worked for lead and fluorspar. Backdale Mine, more quarry than mine can clearly be seen.

Bramley Wood

You now go back into woodland again and follow the path easily to a gate and stile on the right. Once through this, turn left along a good track, which soon reaches a road. Here bear left and then go right, through a rickety gate, into Bramley Wood. There are glimpses of Chatsworth, the Eastern Edges and Sir William Hill, but more intriguing are the occasional small square blocks of concrete by the path. They appear to be boundary markers, but to what purpose? As you walk along there is an increasing sense of height and then the realisation, as Calver appears below, that the descent is going to be short and steep.

The path begins to descend. At the second signpost, go left down a track that steepens increasingly as you descend. At the next signpost go right, leaving the track and dropping steeply through scrub to a stile into open fields. Continue to descend, soon crossing a muddy area by a spring. Climb up from the spring, bearing slightly right to the hawthorn and stile in the wire fence, then alongside the wall to a gap. Bear right, through the gap and continue along the backs of the houses to the point where a stile on the left drops into what looks like a private drive. Follow the drive to the village main street and there turn right. Look out for the outlet of Calver Sough on your right, just at the point where the footpath for Bubnell leaves the road. Continue on the street to the main road. Cross it and go down the footway past the craft centre, over the old bridge and so to the Bridge Inn.

Walk 6. Cat & Fiddle

The Route: Danethorn Hollow, Three Shire Heads, Danebower Quarries, Danebower Hollow.

Distance: 6 miles. Allow 3 hours exclusive of stops.

Start: The Cat & Fiddle, (Grid reference 001719)

Map: OS Explorer OL 24 – The Peak District, White Peak Area.

How to get there:

By bus – *There is a daily service, 58, from Macclesfield to Buxton and an additional 57 on Sunday morning. Ask for The Cat & Fiddle.*

By car – *From Buxton or Macclesfield, travel on the A537 to The Cat & Fiddle. There is a small amount of public car parking opposite the pub.*

The Pub

The Cat & Fiddle public house (tel: 01298 23364) dates from 1831 to serve the needs of thirsty and somewhat tired travellers on a new turnpike road opened in that year between Macclesfield and Buxton. The previous toll road dates from 1759 and not far from the pub is a section of the old route, known as Stonyway, where you can see an original stone milepost indicating distances to Macclesfield and London.

The pub was built by a Macclesfield banker, John Ryles, and has remained as one of the highest public houses in the land ever since. The pub is divided into a lounge and public bar. The latter is a favourite for walkers and bikers who take a break here. Not only will you find Robinson's Best Bitter and Old Stockport on hand-pull, but very often a Robinson's seasonal ale. There's always a superb cup of coffee here too.

The Cat & Fiddle is open all day, every day with the exception of Mondays when it closes at 5.00pm (1700 hours). Food is served from 11.00am onwards but please note that times vary according to the season. Families are welcome and you will be guaranteed spectacular views on a clear day. It is certainly atmospheric when there's snow on the ground or the cloud is lying low.

The Walk

The walk is moderately demanding in that there are climbs and some steep descents which need to be taken into account in your reckoning. From the entrance to the Cat & Fiddle, cross the main road to the bus stop and viewpoint. Keep ahead on the main track that leads away from the pub across open moorland. Go through a gate and continue on this track as it bends left.

However, be on the lookout for the Peak and Northern Footpath sign indicating a lesser path off to the right to Wildboarclough via Cumberland Brook. This path leads to the head of a stream and follows the clough down, steeply in places, to a gathering ground for waters. The path levels at this point and reaches a junction. Continue ahead as signposted to Three Shire Heads as the other path bears off right to follow the Cumberland Brook as it tumbles down to Wildboarclough.

Your track begins to rise alongside a clough to a summit and then descends more gently towards the main A54 road. Cross the road with due care and attention – and we mean this. Step neatly over the crash barrier to descend to a ladder stile. Keep ahead and cross a stone step-stile. In this next field head left down the field to the corner; you will see Holt Farm is ahead. However, you keep right on a green track to reach a gateway on the left through which you pass.

River Dane

Keep company with the dry-stone wall to your left at first and then follow it as it bends right into the valley of the infant River Dane. Go through a gate and continue ahead. The path continues to Three Shire Heads. Cross the bridge and continue ahead through the gate. You begin to rise alongside the stream to your right. On reaching a junction and bridge keep left here.

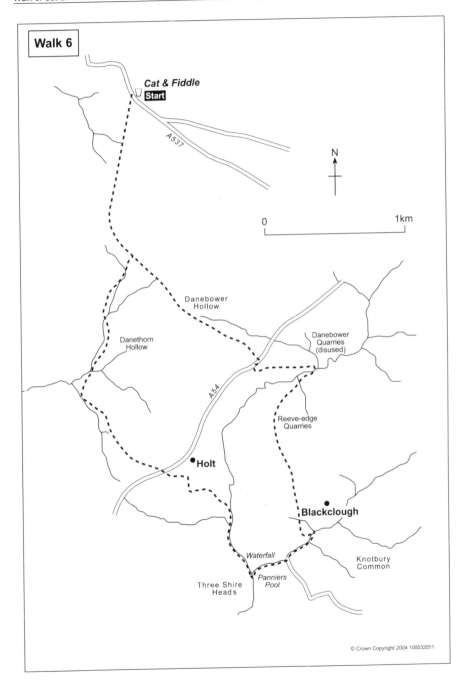

Walk 6

Cat & Fiddle
Start

A537

N

0   1km

Danebower
Hollow

Danethorn
Hollow

Danebower
Quarries
(disused)

A54

Reeve-edge
Quarries

●Holt

●Blackclough

Waterfall

Panniers
Pool

Three Shire
Heads

Knotbury
Common

© Crown Copyright 2004 100032053

As you progress along this track look out for a section of dry-stone wall on your left. Be vigilant here for there's a little green path off to the left beforehand. This inconspicuous little track rises and then curves right across the moorland. In fact, it offers a pleasant and quiet stroll across the head of Blackclough, where there is rough ground, to the lower slopes of Reeve Edge. The track peters out to a less clear path, but your way is ahead as the wall of an old enclosure peels off to the right.

Danebower Quarries

The path comes to a gateway in a wall where you join a wider track again. Go left on it to the remains of the disused Danebower quarries. The nature of the terrain changes somewhat to more of an urban heritage trail winding its way, in a horseshoe shape through the spoil heaps. It splits before the spoil heaps and you keep to the left fork, signposted for the Dane Valley Way (DVW). The path then curves right and squeezes between the mounds before dipping left to a ford before climbing through piles of rubble again. Bear left again to weave your way through the spoil to the hillside, rising all the while to a more distinct track which continues ahead to a gateway and stile before a solitary old chimney. On crossing the stile, go immediately right; it is a stiff climb up the bank to the road. Cross the crash barrier and road, gingerly if you are to survive, to join a bridleway to Danebower Hollow

Danebower Hollow

The track is wide and has been resurfaced to accommodate cyclists too. It rises beneath Whetstone ridge and bends to the right. You reach the point where you branched off on the outward leg. Keep ahead and follow the track back to The Cat & Fiddle public house. On a clear day it is a very easy landmark and the mast near to the pub is a reminder of how ugly features can affect the natural landscape. When cloud cover is low or there's snow in the air the pub is obscured, so be sure to keep on the track. Anyway, if you have chosen the right day this last section will afford good views across Cheshire and enable you to dream the idle thoughts of a rambler before refreshment is close to hand.

Walk 7. Chapel-en-le-Frith

The Route: Burrfields, Bowden Hall, Wash, Shireoaks, Breckhead, Breckend, Chapel Milton, Bridgeholm Green, The Crosses.

Distance: 5 miles. Allow 3 hours exclusive of stops.

Start: The Market Place, Chapel-en-le-Frith (Grid Reference 057808)

Map: OS Explorer OL 1 – The Peak District, Dark Peak Area.

How to get there:

By bus – *Daily service, bus 199 from Manchester Airport, Stockport and Buxton and what a service this is: top form when not affected by congestion. There are other less frequent bus services from Castleton (200), Chesterfield (X67), and Chinley (189/190).*

By car – *Travel on the A6 road between Buxton and Stockport. Chapel-en-le-Frith is signposted from the by-pass.*

The Pub

As you might expect there are a number of public houses nestled around the market place but our preference is The Roebuck (tel: 01298 812274), an old coaching inn (known in previous times as Old Hall). This is reflected in a painting in the front lounge and the coaching horns that adorn the oak beams of this historic pub. There are also a number of photographs of the town in earlier times and other artefacts that herald the history of the town. In fact, the pub retains a traditional feel to it and always seems very relaxing but especially so in winter when there is a real fire in the grate. There is a small bar to the left of the main entrance, the main lounge area to the right and a back bar.

The Roebuck Inn is open all day every day and serves Tetley Mild (unusual for this area), Tetley Bitter and Courage Directors on hand –pull. Food is served from 12 noon until 2pm daily (3pm on Sunday). Families are welcome and dogs too. Accommodation will be available in the future.

The Walk

The walk is easy to moderate with a few climbs only. Start from the water trough in the Market Place, adjacent to the Market Cross and the nearby stocks. In fact, the Market Place has an almost entire medieval kit and a market on Thursday, presumably minus dancing bear and flying chickens. It is a very compact quarter but does not suffer from traffic like the main street despite the by-pass. With your back to the trough or main road, go right to walk along Market Place and, at the corner with Church Brow, continue ahead to walk down a path which runs alongside the churchyard to a road.

Black Hole

Look back at Chapel-en-le-Frith church; it is an impressive place of worship in such a commanding position above the town. Perhaps, this is why the Roundheads decided to incarcerate as many as 1500 Scottish Royalists in the building during a dark period of the Civil War. On their release, forty-four were found dead and many more barely alive. Since this deed, the church has been known as the Black Hole of Derbyshire.

Cross the road to find a path leading off between a hedge and fence to a road in a small estate built in recent years. Go left and in less than 50 metres go right to walk down another path by Safeway supermarket to a bridge across a stream. Once over this, go along another path to reach the A624. Cross over and enter a road, The Crescent, which curves away to the left. You, however, keep ahead between houses on another enclosed path.

Proceed down steps and cross a narrow lane. Go up steps by a tall Victorian dwelling and keep ahead to pass by a factory into open countryside with a view of Chinley Churn to the left and Mount Famine. The path soon reaches the main A6 road and this is the scary part. Please be vigilant when crossing!

On the other side, walk down steps and keep ahead. Pass between a pool on the left and Bowden Hall on the right, seen through a plantation of slender beech trees. The path exits by a white gate onto a road.

Turn left and in approximately 50m go right as signposted through woodland to cross a trickle of a stream to reach a stone step-stile. Cross this and then head left to cut across the field to another stone step-stile. Once over, follow the path as it continues ahead to the left of a stable and crosses a stile by a barred gate. Proceed ahead to cross another. The path now keeps company with a line of hawthorns and holly on the left and then drops to a back lane at the end.

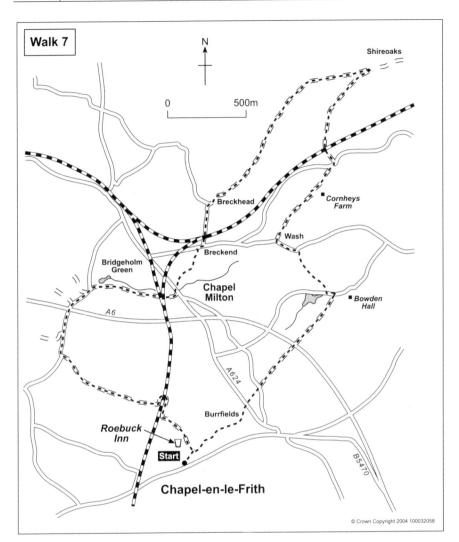

Slab Bridge

Go left here by the few houses which comprise the quiet hamlet of Wash. The road descends to a bridge. Do not cross this but go right by a cottage at the signpost into rough pasture. Continue ahead, with the stream to the left and Cornheys Farm comes into view. Go through wet ground and then edge closer to the brook. Cross the fine stone-slab bridge on the left and then turn right to cross a drive. Go over a stile,

Railway underbridge, Wash

which sometimes has a warning about bulls – not that we have ever
seen one in this field. Look before entering and, if all clear, head away
from the stream to exit by way of gap-stile next to a gate in the field
corner.

Another World

Once on the road, look for a gap-stile on the other side and walk towards
the horseshoe-shaped tunnel beneath the Manchester to Sheffield railway line. It is almost as if you step out into a different world as the landscape seems wilder and more windswept. The path follows the wall and
is soon waymarked, left, to a stile by a holly tree. Once over, head very
slightly right up the field bank to the top left-hand corner, where two
fine stone gateposts stand.

Continue ahead beneath hawthorn boughs on what was an old track.
Follow this to a point well before the isolated farmstead of Shireoaks.
You approach a gateway and ruins of an old barn on the right where you
turn left, yes left, to follow the drive away from the farm. This aggregate
track climbs gently through the field and you are now on the return leg
to Chapel-en-le-Frith, which can be seen in the distance. The views
across to Combs Moss are exceptional.

Breckhead

Once through the gateway, take a left fork and the route along this green way is straightforward enough. You pass what looks like a platelayers' hut and then the track runs down the hillside, with a succession of gates and a wall to the right, to the hamlet of Breckhead. The track curves left here, and then right to reach a metalled road. Turn left and walk down to cross the railway bridge and, at the junction, bear right. This little stretch soon leads to a lower junction. Bear left on the lower road. Pass through a squeeze stile after a few paces. The path runs ahead, and not up the embankment, into a small enclosure where it cuts across to a white house and a lane. Turn right and follow this down to the Cross Keys public house at Chapel Milton.

Double Viaduct

The impressive double viaduct of the quarry line to Buxton stands high above you. There's often a quarry train sitting on one of the arms waiting for clearance to proceed onto the main line. Cross the road and turn left. Within a few paces bear right along a path beneath the arches. Climb over a ladder stile. The path leads to the right, near to the stream, and soon approaches an old mill complex, which now houses a number of small works. Go through the tightest gap-stile by a gate and walk ahead through the yard.

The old Bridgeholm Mill on the right is a now apartments. Turn left and walk up the widened road beneath the by-pass and climb past a farmhouse on the right. The road narrows again and you need to look for a track leading off to the left. Cross a stile by a gate and go straight on along this rather damp green lane. Cross another stile and keep ahead. The old track is still discernible as it climbs to a stile on the right by a gate that leads into a paddock. Cross this and turn left to climb the bank, passing by a farm and houses known as The Crosses. Go over two stiles and proceed ahead. The path keeps to the right of the garden hedge and crosses a stile into a field.

The path now rises to a brow and the view of the works dominates. Cross a stile and drop down the side of the field to a track below. Go left and then right under the railway, a dank gloomy affair at the best of times – and not recommended when there's an aggregate train above. Once through, go right along the path as it skirts allotments before dipping down left near to the works. The path rises by the churchyard and passes between houses to exit on Church Brow. Turn right, back to the Market Place and a spot of tea.

Walk 8. Chinley

The Route: Whitehough, Eccles Fold, Buxworth, Brierley Green, Stubbins.

Distance: 4 miles. Allow 2 hours exclusive of stops.

Start: Chinley Railway Station (Grid reference 038827).

Map: OS Explorer OL 1 – The Peak District, Dark Peak Area.

How to get there:

By bus – *Daily bus service from Buxton and Whaley Bridge (bus 189).*

By train – *Daily train service from Manchester and Sheffield.*

By car – *From the east travel on the A6 from Buxton to Chapel-en-le-Frith and then on the A624 and B6062. From the west, travel on the A6 to Bridgemont and then turn left onto the B6062. This turn is very awkward and is best approached by going to the roundabout at Whaley Bridge and doubling back for a right turn at Bridgemont. There is limited on street parking in Chinley.*

The Pub

The Navigation Inn at Buxworth (tel: 01663 732072) is an interesting old inn dating from the 18th century, when it most probably looked after the needs of the jaggers who led the packhorse trains, followed by the navvies who built the navigation, hence the name, and then the thirsty boatmen who arrived in large numbers at the basin following its construction. The pub has a fair amount of memorabilia to illustrate the rich history of the inn, the canal and the village. There's a main bar, and a restaurant and for many the extensive patio area to the front is a real joy to sit out in peace on a warm day.

Formerly owned by Pat Phoenix, the actress who played the role of the legendary Elsie Tanner in the earlier years of the 'Coronation Street' TV series, it has welcomed many media celebrities in the past. The pub is a very popular meeting place for walkers and walking clubs, so is firmly endorsed by the rambling community. It is a very welcoming hostelry.

The Navigation Inn is open from 11.00am (12 noon on Sundays) everyday throughout the day until 11.00pm (10.30pm on Sundays). It

Transhipment basin, Buxworth

serves Timothy Taylor's Landlord, Marston's Pedigree, Webster's Yorkshire Bitter and ever-changing guest ales. Food is served from 12 noon
until 3pm and from 6.00-9.00pm. Accommodation is available, families
are welcome and dogs too.

The Walk

This is a moderately strenuous walk with some climbs. Start at the railway station at Chinley, at one time a place of importance where people
transferred from one train to another but now not much more than a
couple of platforms to accommodate the Hope Valley stopping trains.
The station buildings have been dismantled and much of the character
has gone. Leave from the station entrance and turn left along Station
Road to Squirrel Green, where there's a hotel.

Go right to walk down the main road, which bends to the right.
However, you continue ahead down the hill in the direction of
Whitehough. The road descends to cross the old Peak Forest tram road,
which was horse-drawn, and probably followed a similar route to the
packhorse trails that existed before. It ran from Buxworth basin to quarries at Dove Holes near Buxton. You will also see the bleach works on
the left; the old tram passed this way. The road begins to climb and

passes the Oddfellows Arms, nestled in the centre of Whitehough, should you require refreshment early en route. You will also pass by a village well, set in the wall here.

Continue to climb the bank on the road. It may appear a little tedious by now, but fear not as once you are past the A6, turn right along Eccles Terrace. At the end of this cul-de-sac go left through a gap-stile by a gate and walk up a greenway and drive. As this bends right you, however, continue ahead along a swathe of grass to cross a stile and enter a field. Proceed ahead along a path to a stone stile, which emerges onto a road. Ahead are the rising slopes leading up to Eccles Pike.

Eccles House

Bear right and pass by the rather grand gateway to Eccles House. The road then passes to the house and arrives at a cluster of cottages and a farm known as Eccles Fold. The road twists to the right and then left. At this point turn left up a tarmac road with restored cottages to your left and on the right. Thankfully, the tarmac stops and after a few metres you leave Eccles Fold by way of a gate onto a green lane offering superb views across to Chinley Churn and Cracken Edge.

Follow this green way until it exits at a stone step-stile onto a triangular patch of land covered in gorse. There's a good view of Buxworth from here and beyond into the Goyt Valley. Take the right fork down to the road and opposite is a stone step-stile. Cross this to enter a large field. Head slightly left down the field, and cross the remains of an old wall before reaching an intact wall to your left which you follow down the hillside to wet ground. Bear right to cut across to a stile before the stream. Cross this and, in the next field, bear right. Head for a point where the dry-stone wall looks as if it is meeting the end of a house gable.

Buxworth

The path climbs up the bank to join several others arriving at the end of a track. Go right down the track, passing a dwelling on the right, and others below. On reaching the road, Western Lane, turn left and walk down to a junction with a wider thoroughfare. Go right over the A6 road and here you will see the restored Buxworth canal basin. This is the terminus of a short branch of the Peak Forest Canal. At one time it was a very busy transhipment centre for agricultural goods, coal and lime coming down the Peak Forest Tramway. There would have been dozens

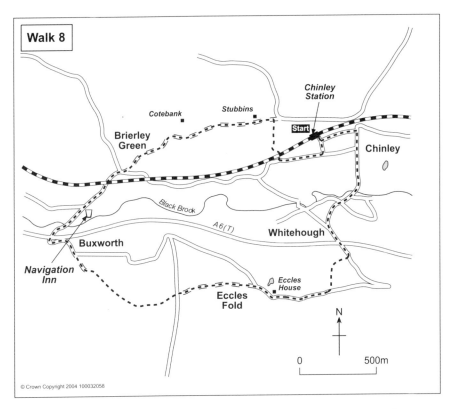

Walk 8

Chinley Station

Cotebank

Stubbins

Brierley Green

Start

Chinley

Black Brook

A6(T)

Whitehough

Buxworth

Navigation Inn

Eccles House

Eccles Fold

N

0   500m

© Crown Copyright 2004 100032058

of narrow boats unloading in these wharfs. Thanks to a group of organi-
sations the basin is slowly but surely being restored and is navigable
once more.

Petition

On the right stands The Navigation public house, obviously named in
honour of the canal and this happens to be your mid-way port of call.
Here you can dwell on the name of the village too while your imbibing
one or two. It is an unusual name, derived from a medieval bailiff of the
Royal Forest called Ralph Bugge. Thus, the village became known as
"Bugsworth". However, in the 19th century this caused some conster-
nation to the residents including the local vicar who led a campaign
from the pulpit to petition Parliament for a name change, for the village
by the way, and not himself. Parliament acceded to the wish and the 'g'
was dropped in favour of a more refined 'x'. Punch magazine ran with

the story and the residents were subjected to intellectual jibes for a season or two – but the residents remained unruffled and the new name remains to this day.

There is more climbing to be done – so pick up your rucksack and let the walking commence once more. If you are concerned about this, there's a level route back in the valley, i.e. the track-bed of the tramway, which leaves from a point beyond The Navigation and exits at Whitehough. From here bear left to retrace your steps back into Chinley.

Otherwise, follow this higher-level walk; it is good for you. The road rises to a junction by a school and opposite stands the old Bull's Head – no longer a pub. Go right here and follow the main road up through the village, beneath the railway to a spot called Brierley Green. Pass Dolly Lane on the left and, a few metres beyond, look for a track leading to an open green at the back of the houses.

Keep ahead to walk up the green, then cross a stile by a gate. Continue to climb up a green way. This can be muddy after rain. It gives out into a field below Chinley House Farm. Ahead by the bank of trees is Cotebank. Follow the dry-stone wall to the right as it curves around to join another green track leading to a gap-stile by a gate.

Tracks

There is a choice of tracks here, to the left, right and ahead. Go straight on and Cotebank remains to your left on the hillside. The track soon becomes a metalled road and passes a number of dwellings as it runs along the hillside. However, just beyond Stubbins, look out for a well on the left side of the road. Go right here, through a gap-stile, to enter a small paddock. Walk down this wooded enclosure to meet a more prominent path coming in from the right. Keep ahead and the path soon descends to a footbridge over the railway. Once on Station Road go left to walk to the railway station.

Walk 9. Combs

The Route: Rye Flatt Farm, Combs, Combs Reservoir, Combs Golf Course, Down Lee Farm.

Distance: 5 miles. Allow 3 hours exclusive of stops.

Start: Chapel-en-le-Frith railway station.

Map: OS Explorer OL 24 – The Peak District, White Peak Area.

How to get there:

By train – *Daily services direct from Buxton, New Mills, Manchester and Stockport. The best way to access the walk is from the train.*

By car – *Travel on the A6 to Chapel-en-le-Frith by-pass, follow signs for the town centre, then for the railway station.*

The Pub

The Beehive Inn at Combs (tel: 01298 812758) is a friendly village local standing in the heart of this quiet village. The current pub was built in 1864 from the profits that accrued from the railway; the original pub is the cottage next door. The stone was hewn from a quarry on the shoulders of nearby Ladder Hill.

It is remarkable that the pub has survived given the isolated position of the hamlet, tucked away between the railway line and the impenetrable Combs Moss. As well as serving local residents, the pub welcomes walkers, climbers, cyclists and those who enjoy sailing on the reservoir. It is an ideal calling point situated as it does mid-way on the walk. The entrance and outdoor drinking area to the front of the inn are festooned with flowers throughout the season, making it a very attractive setting in summer.

There are usually two beers on hand-pull, Boddington's Bitter and Draught Bass. The inn is open from 12 noon to 3.00pm on Mondays to Fridays and from 6.00pm onwards. At weekends it is open all day. Fresh home-cooked food is served from 12-2.00pm and from 6.00-9.00pm on Mondays to Saturdays and from 12 noon until 9.00pm on Sundays. Families are welcome. Check out the website: www.thebeehiveinn.co.uk.

The Beehive, Combs

The Walk

This is an easy walk with only one climb. The railway station at Chapel-en-le-Frith looks very continental – reflecting its name – but is some distance from the town. Thus, it is something of a lonely station but is well used. It was the scene of a runaway freight train accident several decades ago. The driver, John Axon, gallantly attempted to warn others of impending danger but, despite his efforts, a collision took place in which he died. He was awarded the George Cross for bravery and his deed is immortalised in "The Ballad of John Axon". The station building no longer sells tickets but has been put to good use – it is now a restaurant appropriately named Brief Encounters.

Walk along the platform for trains to Buxton to pass the restaurant and, at the far end, drop down to an unmetalled track. Cross this and keep ahead along a path until you reach the next track. Bear left under the bridge and rise up to an entrance to a lodge. Follow the track as it passes the dwelling and rises up through woodland. However, bear slightly right to cross a stile to enter a field. This follows a wall parallel to the railway at first but you need to leave this to climb slightly left in line with a woodland lying to your left. The views across Combs Reservoir and the Goyt Valley are delicious on a summer's eve when a thin cloud cover creams around Eccles Pike as the sun goes down. You will

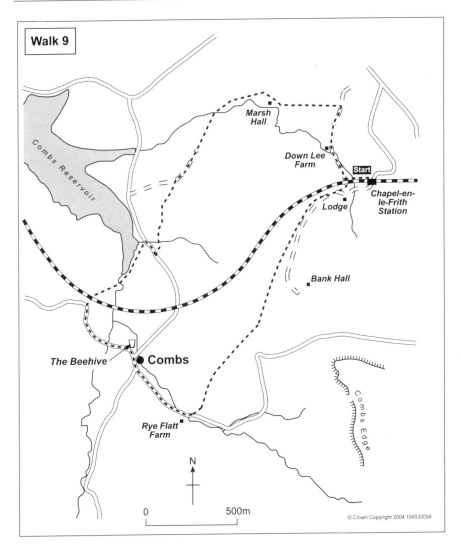

reach a cross path. Keep ahead and climb through hawthorns to reach a stile, which is located near to the top left-hand corner.

Combs Edge

Go ahead to a gap in the next broken-down wall. Once through, keep ahead toward two gateways and you will see barns ahead. There are also stunning views of Combs Edge on a fine day. Choose the gateway on the right and proceed down the hill in the direction of Rye Flatt Farm. The path keeps near to a dry-stone wall on your left. This brings you to a large gate and road. Bear right and saunter down to the village of Combs.

Invention

The route comes right to the doorstep of the Beehive Inn in Combs. This is where Bert Froode invented the brake shoe, having observed the efforts of farmers to slow down using other means such as their own boots. He began to create the famous Ferodo company from these small beginnings. A little-known fact is that Ferodo is an anagram of Froode.

Bear left at the pub to walk along a lane to pass by a post box. The post office has gone since we penned the last edition. As the road bends left before the railway, go right, through a gap-stile. Walk under the railway bridge, and afterwards go immediately right over a stile along a path through the undergrowth to a footbridge. Now go left to cross another footbridge. Those wishing to take a short cut at this point should turn right through a gateway and head to the right of the barn. On reaching the road go right and at the other side of the under-bridge turn left up a well- trodden path leading back to Chapel railway station.

Combs Reservoir

Otherwise, those choosing the longer route should keep ahead through wet ground at the head of a reservoir. The path climbs up towards a fence and you will see a bungalow. Do not go through the gate ahead, but go between holly bushes, as waymarked, then over a footbridge and cross a stile leading onto a road.

Go right for a short section and, opposite the bungalow, go left over a stile by a gate to follow the hedge on the right. Proceed through a gap into the next field. Then walk through the next gateway, some 50 metres ahead, on the right. Once through, head very slightly left, almost diagonally across the field and keep to the right of the electricity pole. Walk into the small enclosure, bearing slightly left to use a boardwalk to a stile. Cross this and enter the edge of a golf course.

The path follows the right-hand hedge to cross another stile and a footbridge. It continues ahead along a slight indent, which presumably is the base of a grubbed hedge. Cross a stile to enter another part of the golf course and go over a footbridge. Now bear right and walk by a stream before cutting over to a stile near the field corner. Once over, continue straight on, with a hedge to the left and continue to cross two stiles leading to a drive.

Down Lee Farm

Go right here on a track, which passes between superbly restored buildings to your left and right. Keep on the track to a small gate and please pass with consideration for the residents. This leads into an old pasture, often wet on the ground, where you bear left to cross a stile. Then, keep slightly left, with a hedge on the left, through a long field. Cross a stile and narrow enclosure to exit at a kissing gate onto a road. Go right, pass Down Lee Farm and walk up the lane to the railway. Bear left before the railway under-bridge to retrace your steps to Chapel station.

Walk 10. Dungworth

The Route: Dungworth, Hill Top, Bents Farm, Load Brook, Beeton Farm, Rod Moor Road, Crawshaw Lodge, Crawshaw Farm, Royds Clough, Corker Walls, Hall Broom, Ringwood Lane, Dungworth.

Distance: 6 miles. Allow 3 hours exclusive of stops.

Start: Royal Hotel, Dungworth (there is on street parking just to the south of the pub) (Grid reference 279897).

Map: OS Explorer OL 1 – The Peak District, Dark Peak Area

How to get there:

By bus – *There is a regular daily service, buses 61 and 62 from Hillsborough Interchange (connected by the Supertram).*

By car – *The journey provides an interesting technical exercise in map reading. Travel on the B6077 from Malin Bridge (north-west of Sheffield) to Damflask, then follow the signs to Dungworth.*

The Pub

The grandly named Royal Hotel at Dungworth (tel: 0114 285 1213) is the only pub in the village and welcomes customers to its bar and side room. The pub serves Tetley Bitter and a guest ale on hand-pull. The Royal Hotel is open from 5.30pm on Mondays to Fridays, all day Saturdays and from 12-4.00pm and 7.00-10.30pm on Sundays. Food is served early evening and accommodation is available. You might also like to travel on the bus to the nearby village of Bradfield where the CAMRA Good Beer Guide entry lists Old Horns Inn.

The Walk

This is an easy to moderate walk. On leaving the pub, turn left along Main Road to pass a turning, Skyhouse Lane. Continue up Cliffe Hill for approximately 100 metres. Look for a stile on the right. Cross this into open fields; the path is signposted from the road. Continue up the fields, keeping close company with the wall on the left until George House Farm is reached. Cross the stile and walk along a corralled path to exit onto a drive and while tethered dogs bark, cross a ladder stile. The path emerges on the farm lane; follow this down to the road.

Go right here, along the road for approximately 100 metres until it bends sharply to the right. At this point, go left down a sign-posted footpath between two gardens to reach a stile and open fields again. Cross a stile and go left here. Then continue ahead through a gap in a wall and walk across to a stone step-stile, which emerges onto a narrow lane at Hill Top.

Load Brook

Go right and up the lane to pass through the middle of Bents Farm, and by another dwelling. At the T-junction at a concrete drive, just beyond the farm, go left down a walled track by the side of the farmhouse. This track is Bents Lane which descends to Load Brook. However, at the point where there are three gates, turn right through the gap alongside the wall. The path follows a well-defined tractor way through a gateway, and then across the next field to finish abruptly in a patch of gorse. Diligent searching will reveal a narrow path through the gorse and a well-hidden stile in the wall.

Go over this, drop down, well almost literally, and walk diagonally across the field to the Load Brook. It is tempting to follow the stream up the valley but this is not the way. There is a stile, on the opposite side of the stream by the holly bush. A path leads from the stile, upwards and beside the wall to another wall ahead. Keep close to the wall and head for a step-stile over the wall.

The access track to Beeton Farm crosses the route. However, keep ahead at this point and rise to a stile which joins a track. Go right here, through the yard. Go left then right by the barn and you will see the farm to your right. Continue to another gateway. Immediately beyond this gate leave the farm road and go left into the field. Follow the wall up the field as it tapers to the road. You've reached Beeton Green Road. Go left and then right at the crossroads. There's a good view over Sheffield from this point, and on a clear day, you can see the cooling towers of Ferrybridge power station, many miles away to the north-east.

Walk along Rod Moor Road to pass Beeton Rod Farm. On the left, the view is down to Rivelin Valley with Lodge Moor and the Headstone on the far side. Ahead, the hills of the central Peak show up in the Moscar gap, where the A57 road begins its descent to the Derwent Dams.

At Crawshaw Lodge (just over half a mile from the crossroads) bear right up the drive, which is a public right of way. The track passes the lodge and through a gate and stile to rise onto open moorland. Still climbing the track swings abruptly right and a grand view opens up ahead. Pause awhile. The eye is drawn across the landscape, through the Moscar gap, to Stanage Edge on the left, Derwent Edge and the Wheel Stones on the right, to rest on Win Hill, Mam Tor and the great bulk of Fairbrook Naze. Keep on the track until it turns sharp left to descend to Crawshaw Farm, seen below. Where the track reaches a corner of a wall a stile on the right accesses a field, and thus avoids the farm buildings. The path through the field is not obvious. Make a beeline for the right-hand end of the farmhouse, diagonally across the field and reach a stile by a gateway to the right of the farmhouse.

Royds Clough

The path emerges onto the farm road again. Here, turn right down the track to Royds Clough stream, a culvert, and you will see Royds Clough Plantation to your right. The track runs to a gateway, but there is a gate on the right, and a path leading into the wood. Go through this and follow the wall on your left until it kinks left. Now make your way ahead and down to pick up a distinct path on a terrace. Throughout there are yellow markers at intervals to guide your way.

The path descends easily through the trees of Royds Clough, with the stream below. There are one or two wet patches, especially in the lower part of the Clough, where the terrace ceases and the stream bank is followed. Eventually, a wall across the route forces the path up and left, away from the stream. Follow the wall, which soon bends to the right, and is reinforced by a wire fence. A recently fallen tree partly blocks the path and means a small diversion into the wood. Be vigilant, for there is a ladder stile just beyond the tree and it is easily missed.

Go over the ladder stile. Head diagonally across the field path, then across the field towards the stream again, finally reaching the metal kissing gate and then keep alongside the fence by the stream. A stile drops you into Corker Lane by steps at the bridge. Go right over the bridge, not forgetting to look over to see the attractive little waterfall. The road rises away from the stream and shortly passes Corker Walls Farm, a substantial place built in 1838, with few apparent concessions to modernity.

Corker Lane

Continue along Corker Lane ignoring the signed track to the right. There are good views down to Damflask reservoir from here. As the road

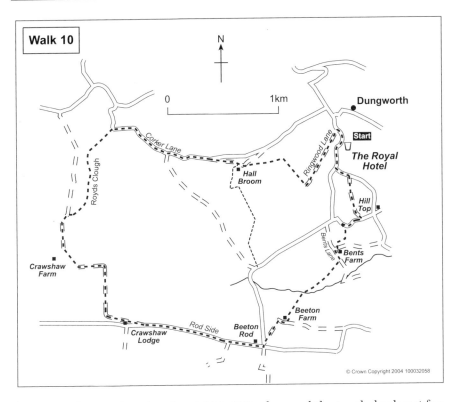

begins to descend again, about 300-400m beyond the track, look out for a well-hidden footpath sign on the right. An equally well-hidden stile takes you over the wall and into a steeply sloping wilderness of bracken and scrub. There is no obvious path, but the easiest passage seems to be alongside the wall to the right. Eventually the "path" joins a track leading to Hall Broom. Skirt around Hall Broom and follow the track down to the old mine workings where the lane swings left. Go through the stile next to gates and continue ahead (ignoring the sign and stile on the right) following the wall on your right up to Hall Broom Wood. The path then crosses a stile to enter the wood. There is a view from here across to "The Rochers", the rocky outcrop near Bradfield, and to White Tor on Derwent Edge.

Sheffield

The path climbs steadily through the wood to a stone step-stile. Go right here alongside a wall and, as you go over the hill, Sheffield comes into view. A couple of stiles are crossed before reaching Ringwood Lane, but it seems no longer to be a lane, as there is only one wall with the scant remnants of a hedge to mark the other boundary. Go left here and the lane soon becomes walled. Where the track goes off right to Syke House Farm, continue ahead through the stile by a gate along a walled lane, at this point, little more than a narrow path. The pub is now tantalisingly in view to the right, so a quick sprint is required along the remainder of Ringwood Lane to the road. Go right to reach the pub, which stands just beyond the Ebenezer Methodist church, a veritable thirst after righteousness!

Walk 11. Edale: Kinder Surprise or Double Crossed

The Route: Edale Railway station, Broadlee Bank Tor, Crowden Clough, Kinder Gates, Fairbrook Clough, Snake Inn, Seal Stones, Blackden Head, Upper Tor, Grindsbrook Clough, Edale railway station.

Distance: 7 miles. Allow all day!

Start: Edale railway station (Grid reference 123853).

Map: OS Explorer OL 1 – The Peak District, Dark Peak Area.

How to get there:

By bus – *At the time of writing there is a Monday to Friday service from Castleton and Chapel-en-le-Frith (bus 200), and a Sunday service from Castleton (bus 260). These services are being reviewed so be sure to check them.*

By car – *From the west follow the signs either from Chapel-en-le-Frith or Barmoor Clough on the A6, then over Mam Nick and into Edale. The car park (pay and display) is on the left just beyond the road leading up to the village and is clearly signed. From the east, follow the A6187 into Hope then turn right to Edale. The car park (pay and display) is on the right, just before the road leading up to the village and is clearly signed.*

By train – *There are daily services from Sheffield and Manchester.*

The Pub

The Snake Inn (tel: 01433 651480) was built in 1821. It stands on one of the last great turnpike roads to be built across the Pennines in the 1820s, following a successful petition to Parliament by the Duke of Devonshire and other worthies. The road linked Glossop to Sheffield but the stretch to the old Ashop Inn, now submerged beneath the Ladybower reservoir, proved too much for the horses. A staging post was needed and the then Lady Clough House was built with a toll bar. The name of the inn that followed was derived from the badge of the old Cavendish family (the Dukes of Devonshire). The original crest was unfortunately removed during the early 1920s. The land now used for the car park was known as "The Little Meadow" and during the last century many famous prize fights took place here.

The inn is open all day every day and serves food from 12 noon until 9.00pm on Mondays to Saturdays and from 12 noon until 5.30pm on Sundays. Beers on hand-pull include John Smith's Bitter and Theakston's Best Bitter plus a guest ale in the summer months. Families are welcome and overnight accommodation is available.

The Walk

Make no mistake: this is a challenging walk. It involves crossing the highest part of the Peak District, not once, but twice. Of course, it can be split into two, but you would need either to position cars at each end, or to pick the days when there are buses to/from the Snake. Best to do it in one day with a good rest at the Snake Inn and to choose a day when the weather is kind as the weather can get rough and the path is not clear on the tops.

The walk starts from Edale railway station. Go up the road, passing the Rambler Inn – too early to stop for a jar at this stage, but when you get back you'll have earned one. When you reach Edale's second pub, the Nag's Head, turn left and follow the Pennine Way signs. The path soon emerges into open fields. Follow the obvious route, in parts stone paved, across a series of fields, with widening views across the valley to Mam Tor and the Losehill ridge. As the path crests the rise there is a signpost indicating Crowden Brook and a narrow trod goes off to the right. Follow this, soon reaching the boundary of open country.

Crowden Clough

The narrow path wriggles its way across Broadlee Bank Tor, then swings gently into Crowden Clough. Crowden Tower can be seen at the head of the clough. The path drops into the clough then begins to climb again, keeping close company with the stream and crossing it at intervals (no bridges, no stepping stones). Where the clough steepens and narrows a path takes off to the left, climbing steeply to reach the main route (that circumnavigates Kinder Scout) close to Crowden Tower. The alternative "sporting" route continues up the stream, eventually reaching a waterfall. In dry weather this can easily be ascended by a good scramble, but if the river is flowing in its usual strength, the dry route up lies just to the left. Either way, make your way up the stream to the point where the edge path crosses.

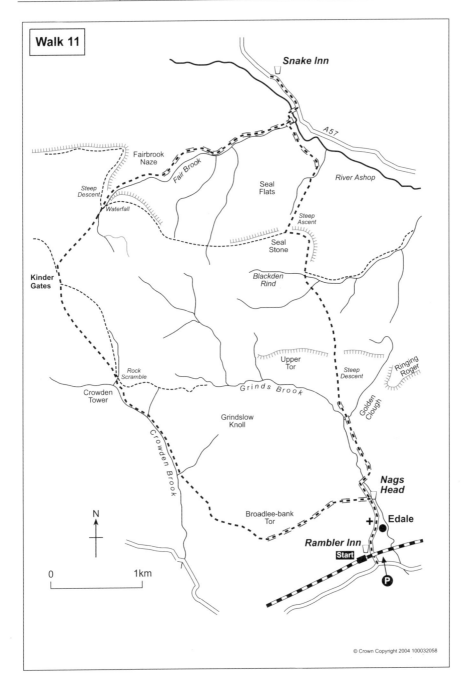

Walk 11

Snake Inn

A57

Fairbrook
Naze

Fair Brook

Steep
Descent

Waterfall

Seal
Flats

River Ashop

Steep
Ascent

Seal
Stone

Kinder
Gates

Blackden
Rind

Upper
Tor

Ringing
Roger

Rock
Scramble

Steep
Descent

Grinds Brook

Crowden
Tower

Golden
Clough

Grindslow
Knoll

Crowden Brook

Nags
Head

N

Broadlee-bank
Tor

Edale

Rambler Inn

Start

0   1km

P

© Crown Copyright 2004 100032058

Three streams join here. A barely distinguishable path follows the middle one, up onto the top of the Kinder plateau. The path dodges about to avoid the peat groughs and boggy areas and progress across this latter day version of the Western Front can be quite arduous. If the weather has been dry, it is easier to drop into the stream bed and follow the dried up water course until it becomes so shallow that you can see out over the top. At this point you should emerge and with any luck you'll spot a couple of cairns to your left. These mark the summit of Kinder. Ahead you should see the one landmark in this otherwise featureless terrain, Kinder Gates. The Gates are two rock bluffs between which the Kinder River passes. To the right of the Gates, you should also see the upper rocks of Fairbrook Naze and these are the keys to your descent to the Snake. If by any chance you undertake this walk in poor visibility, you should be well-versed in the use of a compass and on topping the rise out of Crowden Clough you should set a course on a bearing of 10 degrees east of north.

The Gates

Head across the moor as best you can, making for the Gates. Again, it will be easier in dry weather to drop into one of the groughs and follow it down. Each of these groughs eventually widens out and paths appear as the Gates are approached. Kinder Gates is a good place to stop and take stock. Have you bitten off more than you can chew? If so, an orderly withdrawal is possible from here, by following the Kinder River to the Downfall and then turning left along the edge path. This will eventually lead you back, over Kinder Low to the head of Jacob's Ladder and thus to Edale.

Brave (or foolhardy) souls will be lured by the thought of the Snake Inn. If you are one of these, continue along the Kinder River until it begins to turn westwards (about 250 metres). Now go right, leaving the confines of the river, and going up onto the plateau once more on a bearing 55 degrees east of north. In good visibility you should see the rocks of Fairbrook Naze in any case. Having crossed the watershed, follow any one of the groughs down to the head of Fairbrook Clough, where there is a magnificent panorama over Bleaklow and the Derwent Edges.

The path down to the Snake can be seen below, but the descent to it is steep and rough. Make your way down, keeping to the left of the stream, then follow the path which seems far longer under foot than it looked from the top. Eventually at the bottom of the clough, the valley broadens out and the path bears away left, rising slightly, rounds a bend and then crosses the River Ashop on a bridge.

Go over the bridge and through the wood, soon emerging onto the Snake Road (A57). The Snake Inn stands a short way up the road. Take care, there is no footway and precious little verge. On leaving the pub, retrace your steps back down the road, through the wood, over the bridge to the bottom of Fairbrook Clough. Cross the Fair Brook (no bridge or stepping stones) by the sheep pens and, if the gates in these are open, go through the pens to join the clear grouse shooters' track. If the gates are not open, ford the river a little higher up and then go up the bank side to reach the track.

The Seal Stones

The track rises steadily before swinging right into Nether Seal Clough. Ahead the route can be seen following a wall, very steeply, up to the Seal Stones. It is now you regret having had the second pint in the Snake! After what seems an eternity, the Seal Stones are reached and many people will simply collapse in a heap at this point. Having recovered (somewhat), find the path that bears away eastwards. A short, and easy ascent, soon brings you to the main edge path that circumnavigates Kinder. Keep left and soon reach the contorted rocks above Blackden Clough.

The path swings into the head of the clough and descends slightly to cross Blackden Brook. At the brook, the path forks. The edge path keeps left, but your route bears right, up the bankside and onto the plateau. A clear path skirts almost all peat hags and groughs and climbs very gently across the moor, until suddenly the Losehill ridge comes into view. The path now follows a minor stream and soon meets up with the edge path again. Grindsbrook Clough stretches away in front of you, with a grand view over to Mam Tor and Rushop. To your left is Ringing Roger and to your right, Grindslow Knoll.

You have a choice at this point. You can go left and descend the well-blazed path by Ringing Roger. You can go right, following the edge path to the head of Grindsbrook and then down the clough. You can go straight on and descend a very steep and narrow path, which brings you unerringly to the main Grindsbrook path, just at the foot of Golden Clough. From here it is but a short step down the Grindsbrook "motorway", over the bridge and into Edale, for a very well earned rest and refreshment.

Walk 12. Eyam

The Route: Eyam, Highcliffe, Broad Low, Sir William Hill, Ladywash, Water Lane, Eyam.

Distance: 4 miles. Allow 2 hours exclusive of stops.

Start: Eyam car park (Grid reference 216 768).

Map: OS Explorer OL 24 – The Peak District, White Peak Area

How to get there:

By bus – *There are daily bus services to Eyam from Bakewell (bus 175), Buxton (bus 65 or 66), Chesterfield, Stockport and Manchester (bus X67) and Sheffield (bus 65). Apart from the Bakewell service (which stops at Eyam Square) all the others stop at the bottom of Hawkhill Road.*

By car – *From Sheffield, follow the A625 to Calver Sough then A623 through Stoney Middleton. Turn right in Middleton Dale following Eyam signs, then left as you enter Eyam. Pass the church and at Hawkhill Rd go right following the signs to the pay and display car park. From Chesterfield, follow the A619 to Baslow, then the A623 to Calver Sough, then as per Sheffield directions above. From Manchester and Stockport, A6 to Barmoor Clough then A623 through Peak Forest and Wardlow Mires to Middleton Dale, then left following Eyam signs. Directions then as for Sheffield, above. From Buxton A6 to Blackwell then B6049 through Millers Dale and Tideswell to A623 at Anchor X roads. Turn right and follow A623 through Wardlow Mires to Middleton Dale, then left following the Eyam signs. Directions then as per Sheffield, above.*

The Pub

The Miners Arms at Eyam (tel: 01433 630853) can be found in Water Lane near the centre of this historic village. It is a traditional inn, dating from the 1630s and is steeped in the history of the village. In centuries past, the Barmote Court used to meet between these walls in order to make judgements, hopefully before imbibing too much, over matters relating to local mining rights and claims. The area has a long history of lead mining and hence its importance in past times. The inn is also reputed to have a number of ghosts including two young girls who are said to have perished in a fire on the site before the inn was built.

Eyam Hall

The Miners Arms has a public bar and a restaurant as well as offering overnight accommodation. It also has seats outside, front and rear, which are very popular in summer. The Miners Arms is open all day, everyday from 12 noon until 11.00pm (10.30pm Sundays). Food is served from 12 noon until 2.00pm and from 6.00-9.00pm every day and is cooked on the premises and wherever possible using local produce. Cask beer includes Draught Bass, Stones Bitter and an ever-changing range of guest ales. Families are welcome.

The Walk

For the most part this is an easy walk with some climbs. From the car park (the bus stops in the centre of the village nearby) turn right up Hawkhill Road, noting the fine set of water troughs on the left. These were part of a 16th-century water supply system for the village. You will see other examples later in the walk. Go up Hawkhill Road, passing the museum and a ruined hall. Where the road bends right, keep straight on, up a lane marked with a "No through road" sign. The lane soon becomes no more than a wide track and climbs steeply up Eyam Edge, with occasional glimpses through the trees, back to the village and over the White Peak. At Highcliffe you join the road that runs along Eyam Edge. (If time is pressing you can shorten the walk at this point by turning right, walking along the road and picking up the walk route again at the point described as "Down to the pub".)

Highcliffe to Sir William

At Highcliffe, turn left along the road. Take care, especially for the first few hundred metres because there is no verge, the road is narrow and visibility is not good round the bends. Follow the road along the edge. The road soon bends sharply to the right, leaving the edge and rising over the top of the moor, with increasingly wide views ahead. Soon you reach a T-junction, and there turn right. This is the Sir William Hill road, now little more than a track, but at one time a turnpike route from Sheffield to Buxton. Still climbing gently, you soon reach the summit of the mast-crowned hill and have time to enjoy the wide panorama. The curious name of the road is said to honour Sir William Cavendish who owned Stoke Hall in the 17th century. Not that this is the universally accepted version, for some reckon the name honours Sir William Saville, one-time lord of the manor of Eyam. It doesn't matter. The views are terrific whatever the derivation of the name.

Just beyond the summit, as the track begins to descend, look out for a ladder stile on the right. Go over this and follow the wall on the left through a series of fields. On the left lie the remains of Ladywash Mine, which boasted one of the deepest shafts of any lead mine in Derbyshire. It was latterly worked for fluorspar.

Down to the pub

At the road, go left for about 30 or 40 paces, then turn right at a little gate. The path curves slightly left across the field to another small gate in the corner. These gates are part of a project to make paths more accessible to people who are not so nimble on their feet but who still want to walk in the countryside. You then bear left above banks of bracken before dipping right to another gate above a wood. There are extensive views over Eyam to Stoney Middleton Dale with its quarries and beyond to Longstone Edge.

Carry on along the path, soon bearing right, down a steep bank to follow a well-worn route beside the wall. This soon enters woodland where the path has been greatly improved, before exiting onto the road. Cross the road, go left for a few paces, then right, over a stone step-stile into fields again. Eyam is now clearly in view ahead and if you do not intend to visit the Miners Arms carry on down the obvious path, pass through some old mine workings and turn right along the path, going over the playing fields to the car park. If, on the other hand, you feel like supporting an endangered species, such as Eyam's pub, bear left once in

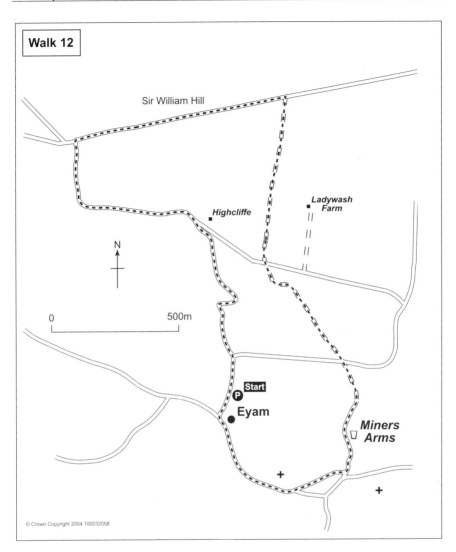

the field and follow the sketchy path down to a gate and stile in the corner, then out into Water Lane, where you turn right. Descend past the Elizabethan water troughs, past the memorial trees, to reach the pub.

On leaving the pub continue down the lane to the main road, where there is a bus stop close by, or turn right and walk through the village back to the car park.

Walk 13. Flash Bar

The Route: Oxenstitch, Readyleach Green, Knotbury Common, Three Shire Heads, Hawk's Nest, Flash village.

Distance: 5 miles. Allow 2 hours exclusive of stops.

Start: The Travellers Rest, Quarnford (Grid reference 033677).

Map: OS Explorer OL 24 – The Peak District, White Peak Area.

How to get there:

By bus – *There is a daily service, the X18, between Sheffield and Hanley which runs via Bakewell and Buxton.*

By car – *From Leek or Buxton, travel on the A53 to Flash Bar. There is a small area for parking near to the pub and stores but please park with consideration.*

The Pub

The Travellers Rest at Flash Bar (tel: 01298 23695) stands just off the main road at a height of around 1518 feet (460m) – a formidable survivor on what was once a Roman thoroughfare crossing this wild terrain. Near the pub is the source of the River Manifold and there are a few seats outside to the rear of the hostelry. In earlier times this was one of the many pub-cum-farmsteads which offered sustenance to travellers on the highways and packhorse ways of the Dark Peak.

The pub has regained its popularity since reopening in 1997. Together with the Flash Stores, these are stubborn survivors fighting the trend to large urban sites. The pub is closed all day Monday, but from Tuesday to Friday is open at lunchtimes, 12 noon until 3pm, and evenings from 7pm; open all day at weekends. Food is served at lunchtime and evenings 7pm to 9pm. A range of hand-pulled cask beers is available, including those from the nearby Hartington brewery.

The Walk

This walk is moderate as there are sustained climbs in the latter section. Leave the Travellers Rest public house and walk ahead to the main road, passing by the Flash Bar Stores. Cross over the road and continue ahead to walk by a bus shelter and along a green verge. Turn left along

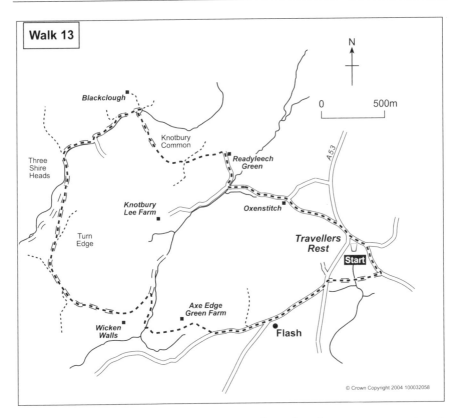

the road signposted to Knotbury. On a fine day there are exceptional views across the Peak District National Park and to the Roaches.

Those of you who frequent these parts will be acutely aware of two points. Firstly, heed a note of caution about the weather. On a day when the weather is less kind, and the cloud cover is low, extra care is needed. It can be difficult to see significant landmarks to guide your way; it is important to bear that in mind before setting out. Secondly, many of the farms were renowned for depositing scrap metal as they often were surrounded by mechanical graveyards. In the first edition the authors made more than a few unkind remarks about the topic. In reality, farming has never been sufficiently rewarding in these parts and throughout the decades the farming community supplemented its income by quarrying, repairs, haulage and scrap dealing. The pattern appears to be changing; some farms have been sold as dwellings and others have diversified into tourism enterprises. On this note, you will see that the route is shared by pony trekkers. The surfaces are not badly eroded by the horses. However, a pressing problem seems to lie with the increasing number of motorbike 'trail' riders using the bridleways hereabouts.

The road leaves Quarnford and begins to descend, passing by a dwelling known as Oxenstitch. Continue ahead to drop down to an isolated T-junction. Bear right here. The road climbs up the hillside to a farm known at Readyleech Green and begins to curve left. Be careful here as you need to leave the road at this point, through a gate on the left, in order to enter a field. Head directly across the field to cross a broken wall and then continue ahead to cross a ladder stile.

Knotbury Common

Once over, turn right along a track through Knotbury Common, and this soon begins to descend, then passes by outbuildings, and a dwelling on the left before dipping more steeply into the narrow valley below. You'll note a few dwellings scattered along the surrounding hillsides. At the bottom, you will need to step over the tractor bridge to join another track. At this point, turn left and within a few metres go through a gate. The track forks but, on this occasion, keep left on a path which runs adjacent to the brook which cascades its way to Panniers Pool. The name is a reflection of times when trains of packhorses laden with panniers of salt or other goods would make their way across the infant waters of the Dane. Another track meets yours and you proceed ahead to the bridge, also known as Three Shire Heads, where the counties of Cheshire, Derbyshire and Staffordshire meet.

Dane Valley

Before the bridge, turn left to walk along a sandy track. At the next gate, keep to the higher route as it climbs gently along the edge of the Dane Valley. The track continues to climb and becomes more made up. It passes old farmstead buildings, and becomes a metalled road which runs through a gate, curves left and climbs at first then descends beneath a cottage. Just before the cottage, look for a track bearing right back down the clough. It is well worn and leads to a wicket gate. Once through, proceed down to an incredibly robust four-directional signpost supplied decades ago by The Peak and Northern Footpath Society, an organisation that has done much throughout the years to keep our rights of way open.

Go left at the signpost, cross a footbridge, then climb to a stile which you cross. There's a good view back across to Dickens Farm before you

Peak & Northern signpost to Flash

take a deep breath and brace yourself for something of a climb. Your way is up the bank, passing through scrub and gorse, towards a dry-stone wall to the right. Follow this wall up the hillside to cross a stile and keep ahead to cross another. In the next field proceed ahead to a wooden stile that leads onto a drive. Go right for about 100 paces and then left through a gap in the fence. Head slightly right up the field to a stile. There are rewarding views towards the Dane Valley. Go through the very narrow enclosure to exit onto a road.

Flash

Steal a march on yourself as you climb, remorselessly, to the village of Flash. It will thus come as little surprise to you that this seemingly quiet village is one of the highest in the land. In earlier centuries it was far busier. Flash was a centre for counterfeiting, and as we say, highway robbery; hence the term 'flashy' meaning something that looks good but might not be all that it seems. The villainy hereabouts became so rife that a crack team of enforcement officers was despatched from Chester to rout the robbers. It really does not bear thinking about as you walk by. On the left is a Wesleyan chapel dating from 1784 and on the right, beyond the pub, is another church and school.

Pass the school to leave the village and walk the last stretch to the main road. You can turn left to follow the wide green verge back to The Travellers Rest and brave the passing traffic. Alternatively, you will notice a stile on the opposite side of the road. Cross this to enter a field and walk ahead, squelch, squelch, until you cross a stile at the next field boundary to switch to the other side of the wall. You still maintain a path ahead until you exit on a lane to the left of Summerhill Farm. The ground can be very wet and muddy during the winter months so tread lightly. Once on the road, bear left for the short road walk to The Travellers Rest.

Walk 14. Foolow

The Route: Foolow, Hucklow Edge, Abney Grange, Great Hucklow, Grindlow, Foolow.

Distance: 4 miles. Allow 2½ hours exclusive of stops.

Start: The Bull's Head, Foolow. (Grid reference 192 768).

Map: OS Explorer OL 24 – The Peak District, White Peak Area.

How to get there:

By bus – *Foolow has daily services from Chesterfield (bus 66, bus X67), Sheffield (bus 65) and Buxton (bus 65, 66).*

By car – *Travel on the A623 and at Housley, just at the top of Middleton Dale, look out for a sign to Foolow. There is limited parking in the village, near the pond. Please park considerately. If there is no space near the pond, there is a small lay-by on the Foolow to Housley road just south of the village.*

The Pub

The Bull's Head Inn at Foolow (tel: 01433 630873) is a traditional, family run pub located in the heart of the village. It is bedecked by flowers for much of the year and offers a welcome to walkers whatever the season or weather. It is a split-level pub with a main bar and lounge area which is thought to have been the old stables (note the equine artefacts) at this one time roadside coaching inn which would have catered mainly for guests arriving on horseback or horse-drawn carriages.

The inn is open from 12-3.00pm and from 6.30pm from Tuesdays to Saturdays as it is closed on Mondays except Bank Holiday Mondays. Sunday opening is from 12 noon through until 10.30pm. The cask beer menu includes beers from the Adnams and the Black Sheep breweries, Shepherd Neame's Spitfire, and Tetley Bitter. Food is served every lunchtime and evening with the exception of Mondays. It is home-made on the premises and therefore may involve a wait when the inn is very busy. Families are welcome and dogs too. There's also overnight accommodation available at The Bull's Head.

The Walk

The walk is moderately easy with one main climb. From the cross in the centre of the village, go across the road (not deviating into the Bull's Head at this stage) and up the lane by St Hugh's church. The lane is signed to Bretton. Stroll along the lane, soon passing an enclosed well on the left. Where the road bears right, just beyond a farm access, go over a stile on your left. The path lies to the left of the wall and makes straight for Hucklow Edge, which rises sharply ahead. Clumps of trees and hummocky ground to your left betray the presence of old lead mine workings. Best not to examine these too closely.

Follow the wall up the field and then climb over a stile at the foot of the Edge. Here you leave the limestone of the White Peak and begin an ascent of the gritstone scarp of Hucklow Edge. The climb is steep, but short. The path makes a bee-line up the hill, soon emerging on the road at the top. Time now to pause and take in the view, which is very extensive. Southwards the whole of the limestone plateau seems to be visible. Away to the west you can see to Axe Edge beyond Buxton. Northwards, Win Hill, Stanage and Derwent Edges dominate the skyline, whilst eastwards the view is bounded by Carlwark, Higger Tor and the Burbage and Longshaw Moors.

Bretton Clough

Resisting the temptation to scoot along the road for a jar at the Barrel Inn, cross over and negotiate the stile. The path now descends very steeply into the upper reaches of Bretton Clough. The tortured landforms to your right are the result of landslips, not mining. The path is equipped with steps, but these are made for people with longer legs than ours. At the bottom, cross a bridge over the infant Bretton Brook and then immediately begin to climb towards Abney Grange.

The climb is initially up a pronounced hollow-way and looking back you can discern the route of the old packhorse track, zigzagging down to the bridge you have just crossed. Where the hollow-way reaches a wall, the path goes left and follows the wall up to a stile on the right. Go over this and then across the field, heading towards Abney Grange. The "grange" place name usually relates to former monastic ownership. Monks who had offended against the strict monastic vows were sent to these remote spots to contemplate on their sins, repent and find absolution in hard work. Not a bad philosophy.

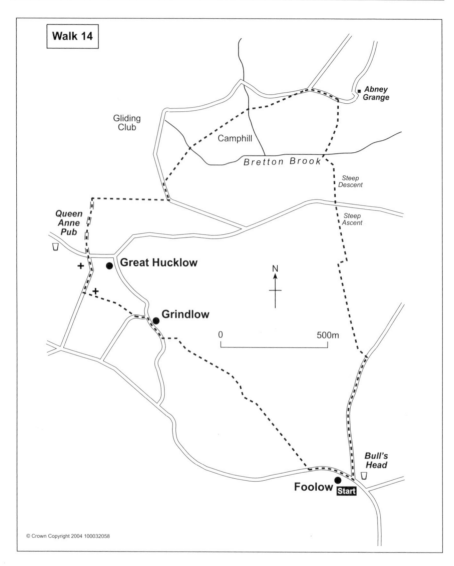

Abney Grange

As you approach the grange, bear left to a stile in the wall and emerge onto a lane. Note that one step of the stile is made out of a stone water channel. At the lane go left and follow the road almost to the junction. Looking ahead, you should be able to spot gliders both on the ground and in the air, for you are approaching the Hucklow Gliding Club site.

Just before the road junction, go left through a little gate and back into fields. Many of the stiles in the Peak District have been replaced by these small gates in recent years. They are part of the Gateways Project, designed to enable the less-agile walker to enjoy the experience of country walking.

Bear left across the field to another of the small gates and then follow the wall on your left, down into a tributary clough. Up the other side, with the ruined wall on your left, over the brow of the hill, and then down again to a substantial stone building. The building was part of the water supply system for the area, but is now disused. It would probably make a good camping barn, given a bit of renovation. The path skirts the building, crossing the headwaters of the Bretton Brook in the process. No bridge here, just mud and stones that move under your feet.

Great Hucklow

Climb the bank away from the stream, soon reaching another small gate, which exits onto the road. The gliding field is on the opposite side of the road and you can watch the comings and goings of the gliders easily from here. The view in the opposite direction is worth a look too, right down Bretton Clough to the Eastern Moors. Turn left along the road and almost at once enter a wood. Where the road bears left, go right, down a steep and rough track through the wood. When the track emerges from the wood it becomes a narrow tarred lane. You follow the lane, passing Great Hucklow school on your left, with views to the right over to Little Hucklow village and mast-crowned Tideslow. Still following the lane you soon come to the main street of Great Hucklow. For those in need of a pint at this moment, the Queen Anne lies just to the right. It is about five minutes walk away. Also worth seeing, just to the right, is the restored cross, reconstructed to celebrate the millennium and the Queen's golden jubilee.

Chapel

Turn left at the main road and then first right, passing the church on your right. A little further down the lane, you pass the Unitarian chapel on your left. This was founded in 1696, rebuilt in 1796 and enlarged in 1901. When this walk was being reconnoitred there was a notice advertising the fact that planning consent was being sought for a further extension. Just past the chapel, go left over a stile (no little gates here), and pass through a series of small fields, with some very awkward step-stiles. The crowning glory is the final stile, which must be one of the narrowest squeezer stiles anywhere – one that is definitely not for

The Bull's Head, Foolow

the "dimensionally challenged". The path wanders through the bottom of a garden before emerging onto a lane. Here you go left.

When you reach the T-junction, go right, passing Chapel House Farm stables. Continue along the road for about 200 metres, when you reach a junction. The "main" road goes sharp right, but you go straight ahead along a walled green lane, passing between a barn on your right and a garden on your left. You are back in the limestone Peak again, characterised by the mosaic pattern of dry-stone walls. This lane has large "causey" stones on the right-hand side, which were for walkers in wet weather when the horses and carts had made the rest of the lane "mirey and founderous" to quote a description of 18th-century Peak District roads. It is a pity they have not been kept clear of encroaching vegetation, because this first part of the lane is obviously used by farm vehicles.

The lane swings right and the "causey" crosses over to the left-hand side. At a squeezer stile the lane ceases abruptly and you enter open fields. Follow the path across a series of small fields, crossing a farm track and then another field before meeting the road just west of Foolow. Turn left here and follow the road down into the village (no footway or verge, so take care – we don't want to lose you at this stage). Time now for that jar in the Bull's Head.

Walk 15. Hadfield

The Route: Holybank quarry, Stonebreak quarry, Valehouse reservoir, Bottoms reservoir, Tintwistle bridge.

Distance: 4 miles

Start: Hadfield Railway Station

Map: OS Explorer OL 1 – The Peak District, Dark Peak Area.

How to get there:

By bus – *There is a daily bus service from Manchester and Glossop – X37,237. There is also bus S37 from Ashton and Glossop.*

By train – *There is a daily train service from Manchester and Glossop*

By car – *The A57 then A628 from the West and the A628 from Sheffield direction. There is limited on street parking off the main road.*

The Pub

Local legend has it that Dick Turpin hid in the village and possibly supped at the local inns, including the Bull's Head on the Old Road at Tintwistle (tel: 01457 853365). As Dick spent most of his career plundering coaches it is difficult to envisage how he had the audacity to call in for a noggin between raids. Evidently, there were dozens of highwaymen of a similar ilk and no doubt the sightings of 1739 could have been one of his brethren who specialised in robbing people as they made their way through the Woodhead valley.

Nevertheless, this old coaching inn, said to have been built in 1573, and located in a quiet corner of the village, has been offering hospitality to the traveller since the time of Queen Elizabeth I – witness the creaking floorboards. To this day, it offers a warm welcome and prides itself on resisting jukeboxes and fruit machines, which distract from good conversation or a quiet drink.

The Bull's Head Inn is open from 6pm-11pm on Mondays, 12-3pm and from 6pm on Tuesdays to Thursdays, and all day on Friday, Saturday and Sunday. Food is served on Friday 6-9pm, Saturday 12noon until 9.30pm and Sundays from 12 noon until 7.30pm. The food is home made and microwaves are banned in the kitchen! Cask beers include Boddingtons Bitter, Draught Bass, Theakstons Bitter and Theakstons XB.

The Walk

The walk is easy going. It begins in Hadfield, a place that is a legend in its own right as 'Royston Vasey', the town featured in the TV programme 'The League of Gentlemen'. Leave the station platform to walk down to Station Road where you cross. By the Palatine public house go right and walk along Station Road to a small car park and entrance to the Longdendale Trail, which forms a section of the Trans Pennine Trail. Walk up the ramp to the trail and continue ahead for just over a mile.

After the junction of the horse-riding and walking trails, walk on to an overbridge. Cut right and right again here to drop down beneath the trail, signposted as TPT West. Enter a field by way of a kissing gate. This well worn path descends to a kissing gate and signpost. Go left at the junction with another path by the perimeter wall of the Bottoms Reservoir. At the next junction go right to follow a path alongside the reservoir to the dam head. Go right again along the dam and at the end right again to climb up away from the waterworks to a stile by a gate. On the road go left to walk up to the main road.

Tintwistle

Cross over and walk up Chapel Brow to the Old Road and on the left is The Bull's Head. After refreshing yourselves, turn right out of the pub and proceed along the Old Road. The houses huddle around Higher Square and Lower Square. Follow the road ahead and pass by what was once a boarding school and onward to pass a Methodist chapel on the left, with a view over Padfield and beyond. Before the next cottage, go left through a gate and up a green lane towards the old Holybank quarry, by the heather-laden banks as the path comes up to the old quarry site.

Open Moorland

The path ahead leads to the edge of Tintwistle Low Moor and out onto open access land, but do not follow this. Instead, at the first crossing of paths, at the old quarry cut back right along a narrow path to a signpost indicating "Open Countryside". Proceed to the ladder stile ahead and cross it. The easiest route is to simply turn right afterwards and follow a

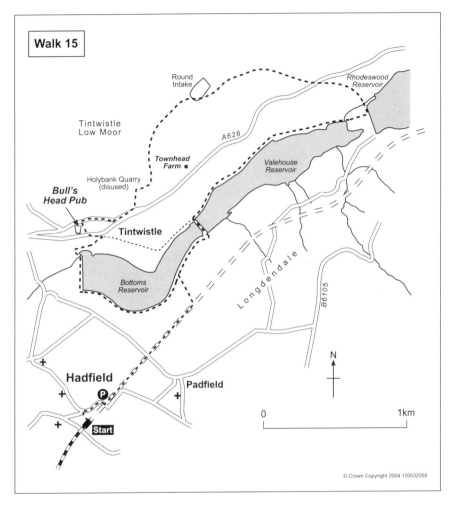

path parallel to lower enclosure wall. For those who wish to gain ground and a good view up the valley, walk ahead through the heather.

Aim to bear right along a path that climbs across the moorland towards the remains of an enclosure wall, marked on the map as Round Intake, although it is rectangular. Now cut right onto a path, which is probably a sheep walk. This rises a little, and then falls to run parallel to the wall lower perimeter wall seen below, then bear right down a steeper bank to join a bridleway.

Valehouse Reservoir

Go left along the bridleway until it reaches a track. Go right to the main A57 road. Cross the road and turn left but within a matter of a few metres go right, down the access road to the reservoirs. Immediately before the dam, turn right through the gates to join a concessionary path alongside Valehouse reservoir, which uses a road where a railway was once laid to build the dams. This runs between the very pleasant Valehouse Wood and the reservoir.

Wildfowl

In winter the reservoir attracts a variety of wildfowl. The road reaches the dam of Bottoms reservoir. There's a choice here. For those who decided not to call at the pub earlier, it is possible to walk back there now alongside the right-hand side of the reservoir on the Trans Pennine Trail. At Tintwistle, you meet the route at the entrance road as before.

Otherwise, those returning to Hadfield at this stage should turn left here to cross the dam and then right at the other end as waymarked with a yellow marker. This well-used path follows a perimeter line above the reservoir, through stiles, but you go left on the one leading through the field towards Hadfield. This a matter of retracing your steps on the path used on the outward leg back to the Longdendale Trail and into Hadfield. The bus stops outside the Palatine Hotel for Glossop, or opposite for Manchester. This is a traditional Robinson's hostelry, which serves excellent mild and bitter from 1pm daily (12 noon on Sunday).

Walk 16. Hathersage

The Route: Hathersage station, Leadmill Bridge, Hazelford, Stoke Ford, Bretton, Abney, Smelting Hill, Offerton Edge, Offerton Hall, Derwent riverside, Hathersage.

Distance: 9 miles. Allow 3½ hours exclusive of stops.

Start: Hathersage railway station. (Grid reference 232811). There is parking at the station, but this is intended for railway use only so please use the pay and display car park on Oddfellows Road if arriving by car rather than the train.

Maps: OS Explorer OL 1 – The Peak District, Dark Peak Area and OL 24 – The Peak District, White Peak Area.

How to get there:

By train – *There are daily train services from Sheffield and Manchester to Hathersage.*

By bus – *There is a daily bus service from Sheffield and Castleton to Hathersage – bus 272 (alight at the George Hotel and walk down Station Road, B6001).*

By car – *The village car park (pay and display) is on Oddfellows Road, just off the B6001 (Grindleford-Hathersage) road. This road joins the A6187 in Hathersage by the George Hotel.*

The Pub

The Barrel Inn at Bretton (tel: 01433 630856) is an ancient hostelry dating back from the 16th century, but it is likely that others have preceded The Barrel on this site during the medieval period. Throughout the ages it has served travellers making their way on a high level route between Sheffield and Buxton. From the 17th century, a turnpike road was built to follow a similar line. It is certainly one of the highest pubs in the Peak District and there can scarcely be a better view. It is situated almost on the narrowest part of Bretton Edge; on a clear day, you can see five counties from this vantage point.

The inn has one main bar, which serves two areas, set out in an L-shape. There's often a log fire to welcome the walker on a winter's day. There are also seats outside the front of the pub so that you can sit back and admire that view. The Barrel Inn is open from 11.00am until

The Barrel Inn

3.00pm and from 6.00pm Mondays to Fridays. It opens all day at weekends. It is a regular listed entry in the CAMRA Good Beer Guide. Beers
on hand-pull include Charles Wells Bombardier Premium Bitter,
Greene King Abbott Ale, Marston's Pedigree and Tetley Bitter. Food is
served from 12 noon until 2.30pm, 6.30pm-9.30pm every day (9.00pm
on Sundays). Families are welcome, as are dogs, and there is overnight
accommodation available at the inn.

The Walk

This is a moderately strenuous walk with several climbs. From the
station go to the main road (B6001) and turn left. Go under the railway
bridge and follow the road down to Leadmill Bridge. There is a footway
except under the railway bridge. Cross Leadmill Bridge, which was
widened in 1928. The original structure was built in 1709, replacing a
difficult river crossing known as the Hazel ford. This carried a packhorse route called the Halifax Gate across the Derwent.

Just before the Plough Inn, at the road junction, go right. Ascend this
quiet lane, with some fine views of the surrounding valley. The lane
soon forks and here you bear left along an even more minor route. This
contours round the shoulder of the hill to enter the valley of the
Highlow Brook.

At the cattle grid, the lane continues, but you bear left down a signed

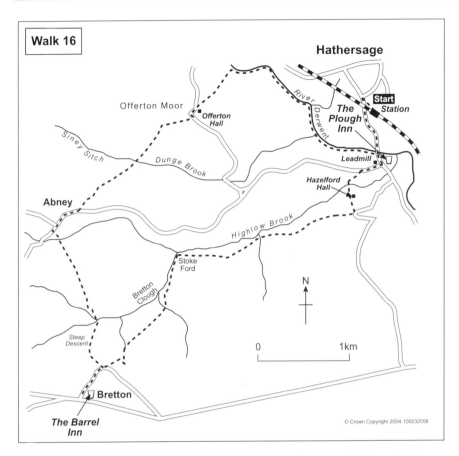

path. This goes through a thorn thicket to a bridge over the brook. Cross the bridge and bear left then right, by a wall. Climb the field, soon passing Hog Hall and reaching a gate and stile. Now climb the rough, walled lane to a T-junction and there go right. Another rough lane leads towards Tor Farm. Where the lane swings into the farmyard, go straight on, through a gate and into fields.

A pleasant trackway, mainly on grass, goes through three fields. There are lovely views over the Highlow valley to Highlow Hill opposite. The suffix "low" is derived from the Norse "hlaw", meaning "hill". Pass a spring feeding into its stone trough and go over a stile into Highlow Wood, a mixture of birch and young conifers. The path winds its way through the trees before descending to a stream. On your right, a simple plank bridge crosses the Highlow Brook alongside a ford. However, this is not your route. You cross the tributary stream by means of convenient boulders and join the rutted track up the spur between the two brooks. Follow this track as it climbs steadily from the Highlow Brook onto open hillside. The view down the valley from this point is excellent, with Millstone Edge being particularly prominent.

Bole Hill

Near two lonely thorn trees, the track bears left onto the flanks of Bole Hill, but you keep right along a broad green path. Bole Hill is another well-known local place name, indicative of metal smelting – in this case, lead. The metal ore was smelted in open furnaces called "boles". These relied on natural wind power for the necessary draught, hence their exposed situation on hill tops.

Follow the path alongside the fence, which encloses a woodland regeneration area. The route soon descends towards the river again, crossing a little side valley and then an area of scrub woodland. Stoke Ford can soon be seen below, but the final descent and re-ascent can be avoided by taking a narrow path on the left. This keeps level, crosses the route coming down from Sir William Hill and then joins the path heading up Bretton Clough. In high summer the bracken makes this avoiding route difficult to use, thus a visit to Stoke Ford has to be the order of the day. The ford is another convergence point for a number of pack-horse routes.

Bretton Clough

As you go up Bretton Clough, the path is narrow, but well defined. There is one difficult spot where a spring has to be avoided. After that, it is plain sailing. Swing into a deep subsidiary clough, losing very little height. Cross the stream and go up the broad green track, which rises quite sharply, passing a ruined farmstead. Continue ahead, soon to enter an area of scrub, where you encounter a very wet section, avoided on the left. The path swings into another deep clough and descends to a stile. Once over the stile you cross the stream on a stone causeway then commence the climb up to Bretton. A series of zigzags, classic packhorse route, climbs the steep hillside towards Bretton. The whole track is shrouded in woodland, but you soon emerge into an open area where there is a grand view across the clough to the higher hills beyond.

Continue up to a stile. This boasts a small plaque. It proclaims that the stile was rebuilt in memory of Hazel Snowden, "to continue her tradition of helping everyone she could over obstacles". Now continue upwards and towards the house and soon reach a narrow lane. If you are partaking of refreshment at The Barrel, go up the lane, passing the youth hostel and thus arrive right by the pub with its breathtaking views over the White Peak.

Hunger and thirst satisfied, retrace your steps down the lane past the youth hostel. When you reach a house on the left (known as Shangrila Cottage), with cart wheels by the door, turn down the driveway; it is signed. Pass to the right of the house alongside a much older and ruined building. A stile leads into open fields.

Head down the field to a post in the bottom left-hand corner, then follow the wall down to another stile on the brink of Bretton Clough. The path now drops steeply, bearing right. Cross another stile and descend an even steeper slope, badly eroded in places, but with steps in other parts. The clough is fascinating geologically. There are numerous hummocks of shale and grit, formed by landslips. At the bottom of the steep descent, the path bears right near a waymark post. It follows a stream down to a clump of silver birch, then bears left and descends further to reach a footbridge over Bretton Brook. Cross the bridge and follow the path, waymarked to Abney, over another bridge, then steeply up the valley side.

Abney

The path levels out at a stile, and quite abruptly, you are back into fields; a complete contrast from the wildness of the clough. Follow the wall on your right and go through a gate, at which point you will see Cockey Farm. Continue to a step-stile, where a signpost directs you to the right of the farm, onto a track. Skirt the farm but, where the track bears left, you go straight on, making for Abney, which is clearly in view. The path runs beside the wall to a gate and stile on the right. Once over this, go left, as signed, and head across the field, making for the right of the trees.

Another gate leads to a track that successfully skirts a stream and a muddy pool, before resuming its beeline for Abney. Abney Clough is away to the right and the track swings away left to round the edge of the clough. Where the track begins to climb, a narrow path keeps right, contouring the hillside below the track and soon reaching a narrow gate. The path now descends very steeply, with steps in places, to a foot-bridge over Abney Brook. Cross the bridge and climb the bank beyond, up to a stile onto the road. Go right here, through the delightful little hamlet of Abney. Beyond the last buildings, there is a step-stile on the left, just by the village nameplate sign. Go over this stile and up the path to another step-stile. Bear right, alongside a wall to a third similar stile. A fourth quickly follows and then the path leads onto open moorland.

The narrow path climbs steadily onto the moor, giving grand views over Abney and Bretton Cloughs and beyond, to the Eastern Edges. At the crossing of paths, go straight ahead, still climbing gently, and soon reach the top of Smelting Hill – another industrial place name.

Continue over the heather moor, noting the piles of stones on the left. These are tumuli, ancient burial mounds. There are extensive views from here to Higger Tor, Carl Wark, Bamford and Derwent Edges, as well as the Eastern Edges. Just past a broken wall, the evil-looking Siney Sitch is crossed on a plank bridge. Dragonflies love the orange and black pools. Shortly after the bridge, a green mound on the left marks another tumulus.

Offerton Edge

As Offerton Edge is reached, a vista of the Hope and Derwent valleys opens up. The path descends sharply and then imperceptibly joins a well-hollowed packhorse-way. This leads across the face of the moor towards Offerton Hall, which is seen below. The path swaps from one groove to another as dictated by bracken and water. Near the hall the path deserts the packhorse track and bears left down the hillside to a stile, which exits onto a lane.

Follow the lane down past Offerton Hall to the lower entrance to the grounds. Here, a signposted gateway on the right leads into open fields. An obvious track bears right, across the field to another gate and stile. Follow the track across the middle of a large field to a gate and stile, near a prominent ash tree. Still on the track, head straight down beside a line of trees, towards the River Derwent. A final spurt leads to the riverbank and a signpost. Turn right here, ignoring the stepping stones across the river.

Goosanders

A well-used path follows the southern bank. In places it is badly eroded and has slipped into the river, so care is needed. Look out for kingfishers and the bobbing of a dipper. When this walk was reconnoitred no fewer than 14 goosanders were spotted on this stretch. The riverside path eventually emerges at Leadmill Bridge, where you turn left to reach the railway station, or, if time allows, call in at the Little John Hotel on Station Road, or turn right to patronise The Plough Inn.

Walk 17. Hayfield

The Route: Hayfield Bus Station, Ridge Top, New Allotments, Otter Brook, The Lamb Inn, Vorposten, Elle Bank, Hayfield.

Distance: 6 miles. Allow 3 hours exclusive of stops.

Start: Hayfield Bus Station. There is car parking, toilets and an information centre at the head of the Sett Valley Trail in the village.

Map: OS Explorer OL 1 – The Peak District, Dark Peak Area.

How to get there:

By bus – *Daily service from Buxton – bus 61 and from Glossop, New Mills and Stockport on bus 358 and 361. Hayfield enjoys one of the best bus services in the area and is easy to get to from the Greater Manchester conurbation.*

By car – *From Chapel-en-le-Frith, Chinley and Glossop travel on the A624. From New Mills Newtown travel on the A6015.*

The Pub

The Royal Hotel in Market Street, Hayfield (tel: 01663 742721) was built in 1755 as a parsonage. However, sometime in the 19th century it was converted into an inn known as the Shoulder of Mutton. This would have been an important coaching inn during the period leading up to the arrival of the railway from New Mills. The hotel stands next to a village cricket ground and there's a lovely atmosphere when there is a game being played on a summer's day. The hotel is also near to the rippling waters of the infant River Sett, which gathers its waters from the legendary moorland of Kinder Scout. It really is a pleasant spot to be.

The hotel retains the relaxing atmosphere of an old coaching inn, with the original oak panelling throughout, and the warmth of a real fire to greet you on a winter's day. There are also seats outside and people love to eat out on warm days or simply enjoy the musical and cultural events of the village which happen throughout the year.

The hotel is open from 12 noon until 11.00pm every day (10.30pm on Sundays) and food is served throughout. Food is cooked to order and there is a restaurant as well as the main bar, where bar meals are available. There is also a family lounge for families with children. The Royal

Hotel is featured in the CAMRA Good Beer Guide and offers Marston's Pedigree Bitter, Hyde's Traditional Bitter and Jekyll's Gold Premium Ale and an additional six guest beers per week. The Royal Hotel offers accommodation – see www.theroyalhayfield.co.uk.

The Walk

This is a moderately strenuous walk and involves climbs and a fairly steep descent from isolated moorland, so you need to be neat on your feet. From the bus station, turn right to walk up Station Road to the main A6015. On your left is the Kinder Lodge public house (a CAMRA Good Beer listed pub well worth a visit). Cross over to enter Chapel Street and follow this until it becomes an unmetalled track which passes two dwellings. The track then steepens and bends to the right to join another path coming in from the left. The track bends to the left by another dwelling and passes through a farmyard where a barn stands to the left. Cross stiles by gates and keep ahead. After an electric telegraph pole, by an old gatepost, cross a stone step-stile into an adjacent field. Now go right and brace yourself for a climb alongside the dry-stone wall on your right. This leads up to stile and steps, which exit on to the drive for Barnsfield Farm. Turn right here to walk away from the farm and to a crossroads.

Pause awhile in order to admire the view back to Hayfield, to Lantern Pike, and across to Kinder Scout. These hills played an important part in establishing rights for people to gain access to the countryside. Hayfield, as you might probably know, was the gathering place for the mass trespass in 1932, when several hundred people walked from Hayfield to Kinder to demonstrate that rights of way across the moorlands existed and that there should be freedom of access, a point not accepted by the landowners. Several of the leaders of the trespass were tried and jailed and only after several trespasses and sustained political campaigning did the Access to the Countryside Act of 1949 bring improved access, some 17 years later.

At this crossroads, bear left to go through a small gate and rise up through moorland parallel with a wall on your left. This peels away to the left and there is a path in the direction of Phoside Farm, but this is not your way on this occasion. You continue to climb ahead and above Foxholes Clough which is situated to your left. There are fine views for miles around, assuming that you have chosen a good day, but there's better to come. You eventually reach a summit on a clear track still

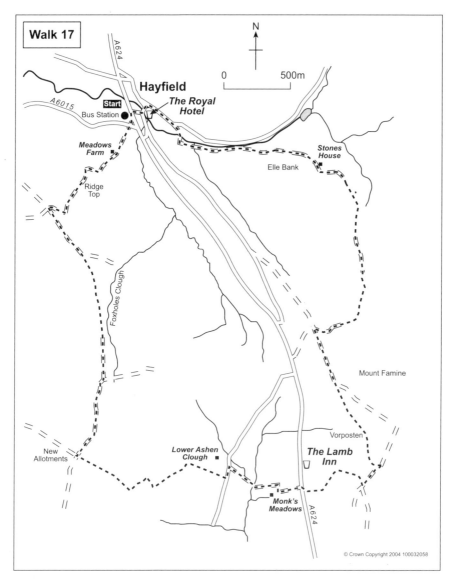

rising near to a wall and there's a signpost at a meeting of the ways. Turn right here and follow the walled bridleway, which bends left, and then runs more or less ahead across the moorland. The township seen to the right in the distance is New Mills, and Lyme Park is beyond.

Outcrop at Chinley Churn

New Allotments

The bridleway reaches a cross-roads at a place known as New Allotments. Your way is left to climb the dip slope of Chinley Churn on this lesser but nevertheless clear moorland path. You join a dry-stone wall up to the summit and then cross a stile. Keep ahead and cross a stile that brings you near to the scarp slope where there are weather-moulded outcrops. There's a bird's-eye view of the valley below and a panoramic view beyond. It is simply breath-taking.

Otter Brook

The challenge is how to get down. There is a path which heads down the slope slightly right and this joins a main route. Look for a seat on the right and old quarry workings beyond – this is a good place to rest. On the main path, go left for about 10 metres and then head to the right, down the hillside again. The path weaves its way between hawthorns and then cuts left to descend more gently. It follows a green track through rough ground. However, do not continue along it to the gateway into the next field. Instead, look for a stile to the right under the tree. Cross a stile here and walk ahead though the next pasture to cross another stile. Keep ahead again and cross a stile to exit onto a road.

Go left and, just before the entrance to Lower Ashen Clough House on the left, look for a stone stile and signpost on the right. Walk down the corralled path. Go through the gate and walk across a narrow stretch of land where a streamlet known as Otter Brook flows (sometimes) to another gate. Once through, keep ahead through the field and go over a stile to a green track. Turn right and walk to the drive. Go left for a short climb up to the main A624 road.

The Lamb Inn

A few metres along the road you will find the Lamb Inn for those in need of a stop. Otherwise, cross the road and just on your right is a step-stile. Cross this and then cut to the right – well, make it more of a leap as the step is high, on the right of an old building. Approach the wall and then bear left to climb up to a gateway. Once through, the path bends to the left and rises through swathes of heather. It curves to the right above a wooded clough and passes through a gate. The green way runs through another gateway by an electric telegraph pole and soon joins a main track as it approaches another gateway.

Stop as you need to go left on this track but do not go through the gate and stile ahead. Your way is on a green way, which curves left to join a wall. This leads up to Vorposten farm on the lower flanks of Mount Famine. It was named thus as farmers considered that their sheep or cattle never seemed to thrive on these slopes. There are two gates to negotiate here but keep ahead and you cross a stile by a gate to join another track coming in from the right. Keep ahead and descend towards old farm buildings. Look for a gate on the right.

Kinder Scout

Follow this corralled path as it crosses a field to another gate. Once through, continue to rise again to the head of the field at a gateway. The views across to Kinder Scout are exceptional. A well-worn path descends to a road but before this, keep left, as signposted, to continue on a green path which now rises again. This rises to a woodland known as Elle Bank and the path forks. Keep to the lower path and this curves left as it descends through the woodland and then bends right to pass by a dwelling, Stones House.

Now bear left and follow this path until it reaches a road. The River Sett is to your right and there's a camping ground here too. Before you reach a row of houses on the right cut down right to cross the River Sett and walk up Spring Vale Road. This joins the Kinder Road. Keep ahead and as this forks keep left to The Royal Hotel. It is time for your well-earned break. Afterwards, go over the bridge and pass between the Bull's Head and Hayfield Church to arrive at the crossing at the main road where you will find horses, cycles and wheelchair users all making use of this superb facility. The bus station lies ahead.

Walk 18. Hope

The Route: Hope station, Netherhall Bridge, Edale Road, Losehill Farm, (Losehill, Back Tor), Hollins Cross, Ollerbrook Booth, Rowland Cote (YHA), Jaggers Clough, Upper Fulwood Farm, Bagshaw Bridge, Oaker Farm, Townhead, Netherhall Bridge, Hope station.

Distance: 10 miles, (10½ miles via Losehill and Back Tor summits). Allow 5 hours exclusive of stops.

Start: Hope railway station (Grid reference 181832).

Map: OS Explorer OL 1. The Peak District, Dark Peak Area.

How to get there:

By bus – *There are daily services passing the end of Hope station approach from Sheffield (272) and Bakewell (173). There are Sunday services from Glossop, Matlock and Chesterfield (buses 373, 173/4,279 respectively).*

By train – *There are daily services from Sheffield and Manchester.*

By car – *Follow the A6187 westwards towards Hope. The station is 800 metres east of Hope village. Parking is free.*

The Pub

The Cheshire Cheese Inn at Hope (tel: 01433 620381) is a superb pub located on the Edale Road in Hope. Like many of the inns featured in this book, it most probably came into existence to serve the needs of those leading packhorse trains through the Peak District from the Cheshire Plains to the townships in the east of England. The pub's name, for example, is said to derive from the way in which travellers paid for their overnight accommodation with cheese. It was part of the bartering economy and there are still some cheesehooks remaining to illustrate the practice.

The inn is divided into three parts with a restaurant area in the lower level. These are served by one main bar. There are open fires in winter and walkers are made very welcome. The Cheshire Cheese Inn is a long-standing Good Beer Guide entry, which is open from 12 noon until 3pm, and from 6.30pm until 11pm on Mondays to Fridays. It is open all day from 12 noon on Saturdays and from 12 noon until 3pm and 6.30pm until 10.30pm on Sundays.

The inn is known for offering a wide range of beers on hand-pull including Barnsley Bitter, Timothy Taylor's Landlord, Wentworth Pale Ale and beers from the Blacksheep brewery. Food is served from 12 noon until 2pm and from 6.30-8.30pm every day. Families are welcome and overnight accommodation is available – see www.cheshire-cheese.net.

The Walk

This is definitely a walk with climbs so be prepared. From the railway station go down to the main road and turn right. You will have to cross the road as there is no footway on the north side. Follow the road to Netherhall Bridge, cross the road again and go through a stile on the right-hand side of the bridge. Go down the steps into fields and follow the obvious path beside the River Noe, with the railway to your right.

Hope church

When you reach the old mill, the path drops down a few steps, then skirts to the left of the buildings on a track. This soon emerges onto a lane by Killhill Bridge, where you turn left. Cross the bridge and go up the lane to the Edale road. You have by-passed the fleshpots of Hope and missed out on the Cheshire Cheese pub, but at this stage in the walk that is probably a good thing. Time enough later.

Almost opposite as you emerge onto the Edale road, there is a stile. Go through the stile and up the small field, bearing right at the top. The path is now followed easily through a series of fields, with a view to the left to the cement works! You soon cross the cement works' railway line by a very curious bridge. The path wriggles its way past a couple of houses and out into fields again, signposted to Losehill.

Losehill and the ridge connecting it to Mam Tor can now be seen ahead. The path runs alongside and sometimes in, a hollow-way. Continue on this route to a fork, where the route to Castleton diverges left. Your route is to the right, signed to Mam Tor via Losehill. The climbing now begins in earnest.

Losehill Farm

Head up towards Losehill Farm, clearly seen ahead. Go through a series of fields, with only one obstacle, a particularly muddy patch by a clump of willows. There's no avoiding this. Follow the field wall upwards, soon passing a ruined barn and so reaching Losehill Farm. Here you bear left and skirt round the right-hand side of the farm buildings onto the steepest section of the route – so far. The summit of Lose Hill now lies ahead and very steep it looks too. Time to stop and admire the view, which is superb, apart from the cement works. You can look straight up the Winnatts and enjoy a bird's eye view of Castleton.

Continue upwards until you reach an obvious fork in the path. If you are bound for Losehill and Back Tor carry on up, otherwise skip the next couple of paragraphs.

Lose Hill

The final push onto the summit of Lose Hill is steep but mercifully short. On the summit there is a viewfinder and the panorama is quite spectacular, with all the Hope and Edale valleys spread out before you and Kinder Scout prominent on the northern horizon. A well-blazed path leaves Losehill summit to begin the traverse of the ridge, soon reaching Back Tor.

Don't admire the view too much. The summit of Back Tor breaks away into precipitous crags, which are not particularly stable. However, the view from the top is worthwhile, if you have a head for heights. Follow the path down by the fence. The going is rough on a loose and slippery surface and care is needed especially in wet weather. At the dip in the ridge, you rejoin the wimps who avoided the summits!

If you decided not to go up Lose Hill and Back Tor, take the left-hand path at the fork and follow a gentle contouring route, soon entering Brockett Booth Wood. The "booth" place name is common in Edale, but

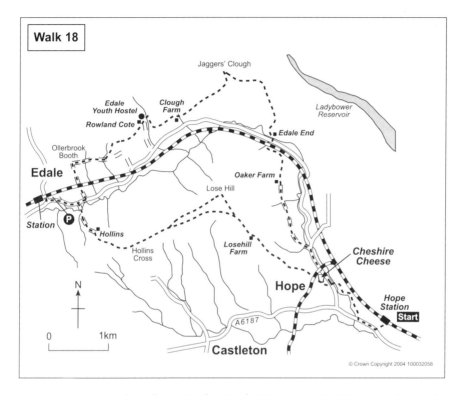

not so common elsewhere in the Peak District. It is Norse and simply means farmstead. On emerging from the wood there is a fine view over Castleton and towards Mam Tor. The path slants gently up to join the ridge top route at Backtor Nook. It is possible to shorten the walk at this point by descending to Backtor Bridge and then along the road to Nether Booth and so to Rowland Cote. However, this is not recommended, as the road is narrow with no verge. Instead, continue along the ridge path until you reach Hollins Cross. Here turn right, but not without admiring the view and orientating yourself, using the viewfinder.

Descend a short way and then bear left, then almost immediately right, following the signs to Edale. Edale village (Grindsbrook Booth to purists) can be seen below. Also note to the right, Edale Mill, recognisable by its chimney. This is one of the few places from which you can see the mill, which is otherwise well hidden by trees. The descent is rough and steep along a badly eroded path, but the view across the valley makes up for it. Eventually Hollins Farm is reached and you now follow the farm track down to the road and there turn right.

By the way, Edale station is only about 500m away at this point. It is therefore possible to do this walk in two parts, with a train ride in between. To walk from Hope station to Edale station by the route described so far is 4¾ miles. To walk from Edale station to Hope station by the route yet to be described is 6¼ miles. Thus, if you are getting tired you can turn left at the road and walk into Edale.

Otherwise, go right on the road for a short distance, passing a ruined barn and then turn left, up the lane leading to Ollerbrook Booth. This crosses the railway and soon reaches the delightful little hamlet. Turn right, following the signs to the Youth Hostel. You soon leave the hamlet behind and enter open fields again. Keep straight on, along a good path with fine views over towards the Losehill ridge, and, for train devotees, within sight and sound of the railway line. Just past Cotefield Farm, the path divides. Here you go left, obeying the sign which asks you to keep by the hedge. At the next waymark post, bear right and climb across the field, making for the corner of the wood. A rough path skirts the top of the wood before coming into the open again. You are now high up the valley side and you remain so for some way.

Edale Youth Hostel

The path soon leads along a well-constructed terrace before swinging into the little clough that contains Rowland Cote, better known as Edale Youth Hostel. You go up almost to the front door of the hostel then round the side and into the clough, dropping steeply to cross the stream.

The path now follows the lowest part of the Kinder moorland, just above the cultivated fields. You dip into and out of various cloughs, sometimes with quite steep descents and re-ascents, but always with a fine view across the valley. Once past Clough Farm, the path descends slightly to join the bridle way coming up from the road.

Jaggers' Clough

Follow this wide track up the hillside, soon topping the rise where there is a sudden view up the Upper Derwent valley. The bridleway then drops in a big zigzag into Jaggers' Clough. A "jagger" was a packhorse handler. This track was one of the main packhorse routes in the area, once called the Halifax Gate. To your left the clough narrows and steepens, ending in the frowning rocks of Crookstone Knoll. Follow the track down to the stream and then bear right along a narrow path to a stile, or 'style' as it says in the stonework. Cross the stile with style and enter Backside Wood.

A narrow but distinct path wriggles its way through the wood, dropping gently down the clough. Soon you cross the stream and emerge into the open. Here the path is frequently "damp" and there are a number of boggy patches. You join the path descending from Hope Cross and pass through a gate and stile on the right, still keeping close company with the river. At Upper Fulwood Farm the path joins the farm track and you go right, then left, following the lane past the National Trust information point and estate offices. Go over the bridge and then go right, leaving the lane. The path scrambles steeply up the bankside to emerge on the Edale road. Go right, then immediately left, under the railway bridge. Under the bridge is frequently wet and an incipient stream runs down the track and ponds here. Follow the track upwards until it swings sharp left. Here there is a stile giving out into open fields. The path across these fields is little used but easy enough to follow. It keeps beside the hedge and fence before swinging somewhat to the right.

At the crossing of tracks go straight on and soon the path joins the farm track that serves Oaker Farm. A steady stroll along this lane soon leads you past the CHA guest house and down onto the Edale road again. Here you bear right. Pass under the railway viaduct, which carries the cement works branch line, and so reach the Cheshire Cheese pub. A short walk on from the pub, look out for a well-hidden stile on the left, which leads down to Killhill Bridge where you rejoin your outward route back to the railway station.

Walk 19. Ladybower Reservoir and Win Hill

The Route: Heatherdene car park, Yorkshire Bridge, Parkin Clough, Win Hill, Hope Cross, Woodlands Valley, Ladybower Dam, Yorkshire Bridge, Heatherdene.

Distance: 9 miles. Allow 4 hours exclusive of stops.

Start: Heatherdene car park (Grid reference 203 860).

Map: OS Explorer OL 1 – The Peak District, Dark Peak Area.

How to get there:

By bus – *There is a daily 273/ 274 service from Sheffield to Ladybower (alight at Heatherdene car park by Ladybower Dam). Sunday services operate over the Snake Pass to Glossop and Manchester (373) and a Sunday bus 257 runs to Sheffield.*

By car – *From the Sheffield or Manchester directions, follow the A57 to its junction with the A6013, then follow this road for about ½ mile to Heatherdene car park (signed on the left).*
From the south make your way into the Hope Valley and join the A6013 at the Marquis of Granby traffic lights. Go through Bamford village and past Ladybower dam to Heatherdene car park.

By train – *There is a daily service from Manchester and Sheffield to Bamford station, but this adds another 3 miles to the walk.*

The Pub

The Yorkshire Bridge Inn near Bamford (tel: 01433 651361) dates from 1826. The name refers to the proximity of the inn to a nearby packhorse bridge. Since these days the inn has flourished as a provider of accommodation and refreshment to visitors to the Derwent Dams as well as those who love the outdoors. There's a main bar with a wood burning stove in the fireplace and a dining room and the pub is adorned with a large collection of interesting ceramics. There is also an extensive garden which recently won the Best Hotel/Pub Garden in Britain organised by the magazine 'Gardening News'. The pub is very thoughtful in also providing cycle parking. Altogether, it is located in a great spot near to Ladybower dam.

The Yorkshire Bridge

The inn opens from 11am until closing time every day. Hand-pulled beers include Timothy Taylor's Landlord, Stones Best Bitter and beers from the Black Sheep brewery. Home-cooked food is served from 12noon until 2pm and from 6-9pm on Mondays to Fridays and on Saturdays 6-9.30pm. On Sundays, food is available from 12 noon until 8.30pm. Families are welcome and there is overnight accommodation, see www.yorkshire-bridge.co.uk.

The Walk

Leave Heatherdene car park by the path at the southern end, passing the toilet block. The path follows the alignment of the Derwent Aqueduct. This carries water from Derwent and Howden dams to the towns and cities of the East Midlands. As you start on the path, note the signboard telling you that you are on the Derwent Valley Heritage Way and that it is 55 miles to the River Trent. As you approach the former Water Company buildings, go right, down a flight of steps, to the road. On your right is the memorial commemorating the construction of the Ladybower Dam and the ceremonial closing of the valves by George VI and Queen Elizabeth in 1945. In reality, the valves had been closed two years earlier, in 1943. Cross the road and go through the gates onto the walkway across the dam. The view up the valley from here is superb, the effect greatly enhanced by the reservoir.

Ladybower

This reservoir was authorised by an Act of Parliament in 1920. The dam is an earth embankment, with a clay core and is designed to hold 6300 million gallons of water. The original authorised height was 140 feet, but this has recently been raised as part of current legislation to cope with flooding emergencies. One happy result of this is that you can now walk across the dam. Work on the dam began in 1935 and took ten years to complete, longer than planned because of the outbreak of the second World War.

Walk across the dam and, at the far side, turn right. There is a viewing platform here overlooking the huge overflow weir, which is like a gigantic plughole. For the most part, it is quite dry, but the concrete steps become a maelstrom of white water during wet periods. Follow the broad track alongside the reservoir with fine views over to Ashopton viaduct, Derwent Edge and Crook Hill. Although this is a motorable track, you will be unfortunate to meet any vehicles other than those belonging to Severn Trent employees or the occasional fisherman. This is a very easy section of the walk, following the Ashop arm of the reservoir right to the point where the river flows in.

During most summers, the western end of the reservoir is dry and you can see the old course of the river. Just before the point where the track swings right to cross the River Ashop, there is a signpost directing you left, up a lesser used track. You scarcely get onto this, before another signpost directs you left again, onto a narrow path, which climbs steeply through the wood, twisting and turning as it goes. This soon emerges into a clearing where there are the remains of farm buildings. When the reservoir was built, the farms on the surrounding hillsides were abandoned and the fields planted with conifers. If you look closely, you can still see the remains of field walls at various points. The regimented blocks of conifers are quite alien to the Peak District landscape but hopefully when the time comes to clear fell the trees, some more sympathetic, natural form of planting will be adopted.

Hope Cross

Bear left in the clearing, now on a wider track, which soon plunges back

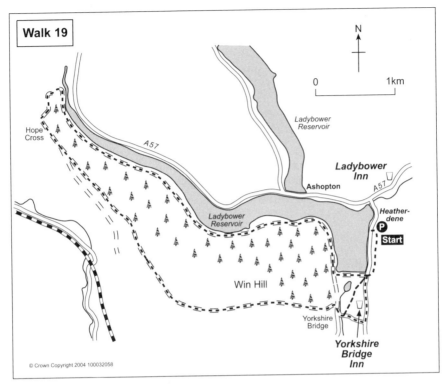

into trees again. Continue upwards until the gradient eases and you reach a stile. Here you leave the gloom of the trees and are greeted with the vista of the Vale of Edale, the Losehill ridge, Mam Tor, Rushup and Kinder Scout. You have arrived at Hope Cross. Hope Cross is not really a cross at all, though there may have been one near here originally. It is a fine example of a guide stone, dated 1737 and carrying the names Sheffield, Edale, Hope and Glossop on its four faces. It may not be in the correct place, for the Edale to Sheffield route crossed the Hope to Glossop route further west, at the point where the packhorse road via Jaggers Clough comes over the ridge. The inclusion of Edale is interesting too. Guide stones were supposed to have the names of the nearest market town and Edale was never one of those.

Leave the cross by the Hope "road", but instead of following this, keep left, along side the plantation wall and as soon as possible go onto the path that runs between the wall and the plantation fence. Follow this path for some distance, crossing a broken stile in the process and then, shortly afterwards regaining a path on the outside of the wall and thus joining the broad track which runs up from the Hope "road" you left earlier. The route you have followed keeps on top of the ridge rather than descending and re-ascending.

Win Hill

The stroll up the ridge to the top of Win Hill is a delight, with ever widening views. The final ascent of the summit rocks necessitates a little bit of scrambling to reach the trig point, but the effort is well worth it. A great 360-degree view is in prospect from here and on a calm, warm day it is a place to linger and soak in the scenic delights. It is not a place to linger when the wind howls and the rain comes hammering out of the west!

Parkin Clough

Begin the descent to the east, where you can see the reservoir below and Bamford Edge behind it. A broad path drops quickly to a step-stile, whence an equally obvious path carries straight on, down into the trees. You soon reach a crossing of paths, where your route is a quick right and left before plunging downhill again, signposted to Ladybower. You now begin the descent of Parkin Clough. This is very steep and rough under-foot, so take great care, particularly if making this descent in wet or icy conditions.

Cross a forest track and continue down beside the deepening clough, still on a steep, rough path through trees. At length you reach a short, level stretch. This was the railway line, constructed between 1901 and 1902 for the building of Derwent and Howden dams. On their comple-tion in 1914, it was demolished, only to be rebuilt again in 1934 for the construction of Ladybower dam. The line finally closed and was lifted in 1946. This lower section is now a walking and cycling route – much of the rest of course lies under water.

Cross the railway and continue down a flight of steps to a lane. Here turn right, go through the gate and down to the road junction. Turn left and cross the bridge over the Derwent. This is the real Yorkshire Bridge. Look upstream to the waterfall and the toe of the dam. Just beyond the bridge is the point of decision. If you are heading for the Yorkshire Bridge Inn, carry on up the road, soon reaching the former water board houses and the main road. The pub then lies just to the left, with the bus stop outside and Heatherdene car park about ½ mile further on. If you are not bothered about a jar, there is a stile on the left near the bridge and a path makes its way towards the foot of the dam before veering right to emerge at the eastern side of the dam, by the gates and the main road. From there, retrace your steps to Heatherdene car park or the nearby bus stop by the entrance.

Walk 20. Linacre and Wigley

The Route: Linacre reservoir, Woodnook, Ashgate Hospice, Broomhall Farm, Frith Hall, Riddings, Wigley (Royal Oak), Birley Brook, Linacre Reservoir.

Distance: 6 miles. Allow 3 hours exclusive of stops.

Start: Linacre Reservoirs car park (Grid reference 337 727). Public transport users have a choice of three starting points; Ashgate Hospice, the Royal Oak or Cutthorpe (Barber Lane).

Map: OS Explorer OL 24 – The Peak District, White Peak Area.

How to get there:

By bus – *There is a daily service from Chesterfield town centre, Baslow and Bakewell to the Royal Oak and Ashgate Hospice (170).*
There is a Monday to Saturday service to Ashgate Hospice from Calow, Brimington, Whittington Moor and Newbold.
There is a daily service from Chesterfield town centre and Newbold to Cutthorpe (Barber Lane), which is the access road to Linacre Reservoirs (bus 89). On Mondays to Saturdays you can also reach Cutthorpe (Barber Lane) from Dronfield.

By car – *From Chesterfield town centre, travel on the B6051 to Cutthorpe, Four Lane Ends, then go left onto the B6050. In about a mile go left onto the (signed) access road to Linacre Reservoir. Beware speed bumps. There is ample car parking.*
From the west (Baslow) follow the A619 to the Robin Hood then left onto the B6050. At Ten Lane Ends go left, still on the B6050 and follow this road for a further 3 miles, passing Prathall and Ingmanthorpe. Then go right onto the (signed) access road to Linacre Reservoir. Beware speed bumps.

On foot – *Linacre Reservoirs can easily be reached on foot from Holme Hall and Loundsley Green estates and from Ashgate and Brampton.*

The Pub

The Royal Oak Inn (tel: 01246 568092), between Old Brampton and Wigley, was known to an earlier generation of drinkers as "Florrie's place" after a former landlady. A welcoming pub, with a patio area for summer evenings, it is closed on Mondays but otherwise open at lunchtimes (11.30am to 2pm, or 4pm on Sundays) and evenings from 7pm. Hand-pulled Tetley beers are available. It also offers food at lunchtime until 1.30pm (3pm on Sundays) – dogs are not allowed during food serving times. Booking is advisable and children over five years of age are welcome.

The Walk

From the car park, carry on down the lane, keeping left where the track from the dam joins. The lane soon deteriorates into a rough track, which soon descends to cross Linacre Brook. At the junction of paths do not go over the footbridge on your left but carry straight on, keeping the stream to your left.

Holme Hall

The track soon leaves the stream and climbs gently out of the wood to be greeted by the vanguard of Chesterfield's housing sprawl. This is Holme Hall estate, an example of Chesterfield's lopsided development that

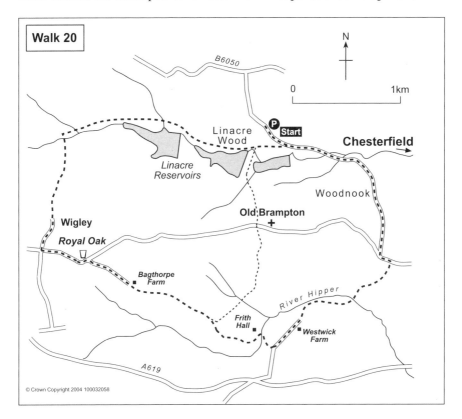

now encroaches on the fringes of the Peak District, swallowing old hamlets in the process. The one advantage is that residents in these estates can actually walk into some grand countryside without having to use their cars.

Keep straight on at the T-junction, with the crooked spire of Chesterfield parish church now visible over the rooftops. Pass by Woodnook cottage, a misnomer if ever there was one, and reach the road just west of Ashgate hospice. Turn left and follow the road for a short way, rounding a sharp left-hand bend. Continue along the road then cross and go right, down the signposted bridleway. At the fork in the lane, keep right.

Broomhall and Westwick farms

The rough lane is fenced and hedged throughout. It dips gently to cross a bridge before rising again to Broomhall Farm, an unusually tall and thin red brick building. At a T-junction, just beyond the farm, go straight on. The lane soon develops into a hollow-way and climbs up to Westwick Farm. From here, there is a good view across to Old Brampton church. The lane now becomes metalled and continues to climb.

Frith Hall and a fine view

At the T-junction by the bungalow, go right and descend steeply to Wood Farm, where the track swings left and descends further to cross a stream. Up you go on the other side, between holly hedges until you reach Frith Hall. The hall dates from 1804 but the name is Norman-French, meaning "forest". The best known occurrence in the Peak District is Chapel-en-le-Frith – see Walk 7.

Go through the farmyard and out into the lane again. Follow the lane up to The Birches, bearing left here. There is an extensive view from this point, across to Stone Edge with its lead smelt chimney and to Bole Hill at Wingerworth. Wadshelf village is on the western horizon, whilst eastwards the sun catches the limestone walls of Bolsover castle.

Continue along the lane, which becomes metalled beyond Bagthorpe Farm, and thus emerge onto the main road right opposite the Royal Oak Inn. If your timing is good, you'll not be able to resist popping in for a jar. Take care crossing the road, especially on leaving the pub, as the visibility to the right is not good and motorists tend to come down the hill from Wigley at quite a pace.

Wigley

Follow the road up to Wigley, making sure you use the footway provided. At the crossroads, go right, unless you have a burning desire to patronise the Fox and Goose, which is further along this road. Safely across, pause to glance back down the valley to Chesterfield. Go along the lane, ignoring the left turn to Moorhay Farm, instead bearing right. There is a surprising view to the left from here, as cars can be seen almost on the horizon at Owler Bar.

Soon you enter the metropolis of Wigley. Go between the buildings and, where the lane swings right into Wigley Hall Farm, continue ahead by the staddle stone (stone mushroom to the uninitiated). Go through the signposted stile, avoiding the ditch. From this point you can see Cutthorpe and Sheffield, but these soon disappear as you descend the walled track, paved in part with "causey" stones. These are usually sure signs of an ancient and well-used track.

Birley Brook

Descend through the woodland until you reach Birley Brook, where the path divides. Take the right-hand fork and cross the two streams. Once in open fields, go right, following the well-blazed path close to Birley Brook. The path crosses a tributary stream via stepping stones, then continues its merry way alongside a thicket of gorse to a stile which leads into Birley Woods.

Linacre Reservoirs.

A distinct path leads through the woods and soon joins the wide track which circumnavigates the Linacre reservoirs. Keep the reservoir to your right and proceed along the track; a delightful stroll through a varied woodland, full of wildflowers in Spring.

The three Linacre Reservoirs were built over a period of 50 years between 1855 and 1904. The first reservoir (the lowest one) was authorised in 1855. The second (top reservoir) followed in 1885 and the middle dam in 1904. The water supplied the fast-growing town of Chesterfield, but because of the lack of any filtration or decontamination, the water quality was not good. In 1909, it was recorded that "the appearance of the water was such that the poor used it as soup, the middle class for washing clothes and the elite for watering their gardens".

Walk past the Upper Dam and Middle Dam and soon reach the Lower Dam. Bear left here, up the track to the lane, then left again to reach the car park.

Walk 21. Little Hayfield

The Route: Church Mill, near Blackshaw Farm, Laneside Farm, Rowarth, Long Lee Farm, Lantern Pike, Upper Cliffe Farm, Little Hayfield.

Distance: 4 miles. Allow 2 hours exclusive of stops.

Start: The Lantern Pike public house (Grid reference 034883).

Map: OS Explorer OL 1 – The Peak District, Dark Peak Area.

How to get there:

By bus – *Daily service from Buxton and Glossop – 61, New Mills and Stockport (358 or 361). Hayfield enjoys one of the best bus services in the area and is easy to get to from the Greater Manchester conurbation.*

By car – *From Chapel-en-le-Frith, Chinley and Glossop travel on the A624. From New Mills Newtown travel on the A6015, then the A624. There is very limited on street parking in the village so please park considerately. Recommended to park at Hayfield Bus Station and catch the 61 or 361 bus – it is no more than a five-minute ride up the valley.*

The Pub

The Lantern Pike (tel: 01663 747590) used to be a farm, and in the first instance, probably became known as The New Inn from 1852 when the turnpike road between Glossop and Buxton was upgraded. However, in recognition of the beacon on the nearby hillside (coming your way soon) the pub changed its name accordingly. The pub is adorned with other snippets of local history and pictorial evidence of times past. It was, for example, the scene of a dastardly deed in 1927 when the then landlady was murdered. The case achieved national importance and Scotland Yard sent one of its finest men north to solve it. Some say that this dear landlady haunts the pub to this day but have no fear for atmosphere is very convivial. The creator of 'Coronation Street' also used to frequent the pub and he spent many hours working on the concept at the pub; many of the actors came to visit in the early years of the TV series.

Needless to say, there's a warm welcome for walkers at The Lantern

The Lantern Pike Inn

Pike. There's one main room divided into drinking areas and a restaurant. There's often a roaring fire in winter, which brings cheer to the heart, and warmth to the toes on a chilly day. The Lantern Pike opens every day from 12 noon through to closing time. It serves Boddington's Bitter, Timothy Taylor's Landlord and Caledonian Deuchar's IPA on hand-pull. Food is served from 12 noon until 9pm every day. Families are welcome and overnight accommodation is available – see www.lanternpikeinn.co.uk.

The Walk

This is a moderate walk with some climbs. Start the walk from The Lantern Pike Inn by turning right to walk in the direction of Hayfield. Do not turn immediately right by the telephone kiosk, but take the next right turn, Slack Lane, and follow the lane down to the old Church Mill complex, which has been refurbished as apartments. As the road bends left, cross the bridge on the right across the brook, just at the end the building. The path leads up to a stile and then bears left up the bank, following a line of stone slabs to join a row of hawthorns. It then bears slightly right (not the immediate right turn to a house) up the field to cross another stile near to another dwelling.

Crossroads

Cut across the drive at this point and head in a similar direction over a stile and walk up the hill. The well-defined path climbs remorselessly upwards and above a wood to cross another stile. Bear right to follow a path alongside a dry-stone wall on the right, which eventually eases away to meet a walkers' crossroads. Do not trust the directions, however, as the post is sometimes turned by mischievous persons to confuse the unsuspecting rambler.

Your way is left to Wethercotes. The track rises up and through a gate and then continues ahead until you reach a junction. Go right here to pass Laneside Farm. The road continues ahead to the hamlet of Rowarth where you might also decide to call at 'The Little Mill at Rowarth' on the left. This was at one time a candlewick mill and a restored waterwheel attests to the past. It is open all day, offers a wide range of beers and home-cooked food.

Rowarth

Just beyond The Little Mill, as the road bends left go right on a track signposted as a footpath. About 50 metres beyond the buildings on the right, go right on a narrow path through undergrowth to a footbridge over a stream. Care is needed on this section. Cross the bridge and go slightly left to rise up the field and alongside a row of hawthorns. Look for a footbridge on the left in a dip. Go over this and climb ahead through rough ground to the left of Long Lee farm. Go through a small gate and then bear slightly right to cross a stone step-stile. Now go right to cross another stone step-stile and then turn to the left.

Leave the farm behind and follow a dry-stone wall to your left as it rises with a slope but look out for a stile on the left. Go over this and descend, slightly right, down the field. Cross the stile into the next field and head in a similar direction. You can see Bulshaw Farm across the other side of the shallow valley. Cross a wall where it is broken down and enter a very large enclosure that is on the spring line and can be very wet. Continue ahead to cross the dip and once through this wet area head slightly left up towards the corner where you can just about see the signpost encountered earlier.

Lantern Pike

At the signpost walk ahead this time to cross the field in a similar direction, but this eventually curves right to a gate. The path is well worn and

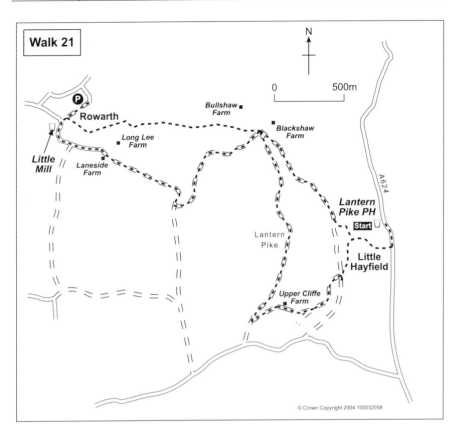

the Lantern Pike (the hill, not the pub) is ahead. Go through the gate onto National Trust land and keep straight on if you'd like to climb up to the monument. Long ago, in times of war and distress, a bonfire would be lit here to spread the message of danger across the land. Such a beacon was lit to warn of the Spanish Armada coming and in recent years this was celebrated with a re-enactment of the event.

Those feeling less energetic should keep to the lower level path which skirts the hill. From the monument or the lower path, make your way to the gate exit in the lower left-hand corner. The view across to Hayfield and beyond is exceptional. You can see the shape of the basin and why mills developed in the Sett Valley with the flow of the streams.

Birch Vale

The path joins a track and continues down the hill to become a lane above the Sett Valley. Bear left at the first junction, as signposted, towards Upper Cliffe Farm. Walk along the drive but as you approach the entrance dip to the right as waymarked and then walk ahead through a field adjacent to the farm. At the end of the walled orchard cut right and immediately left over a stile. Proceed ahead over another stile and now you have excellent views over Hayfield and Kinder. Descend slightly left down the hillside, through gorse to join another lower path. Keep ahead on this with a wall to the right. Cross the stile and keep ahead until you reach a lane. Now cut back on yourself and a track runs down to the Church Mill complex. Retrace your steps back to the centre of the hamlet and The Lantern Pike Inn for a well-deserved rest.

Walk 22. Millthorpe

The Route: Millthorpe, Hallin Wood, Moorhall, Shillito Wood, Ramsley, Little Barbrook Reservoir, Car Top, Smeekley Wood, Eweford Bridge, Millthorpe.

Distance: 7¼ miles. Allow 3 hours exclusive of stops.

Start: Lay-by parking on Holmesfield Road at Millthorpe (adjacent to the Royal Oak) (Grid reference 317 764), alternative parking at Shillito Wood car park (Grid reference 295 748).

Map: OS Explorer OL 24 – The Peak District, White Peak Area.

How to get there:

By bus – *Daily service from Chesterfield and Holmesfield to Millthorpe, bus 89, (connections from Sheffield at Holmesfield).*
Daily services from Sheffield, the Potteries, Leek, Buxton and Bakewell call at Car Top (X18).

By car – *From Chesterfield follow the B6051 through Barlow to Millthorpe. Turn right just before the Royal Oak to reach the parking area. From Sheffield go to Owler Bar then follow the B6051 down to Millthorpe. Turn left just beyond the Royal Oak to reach the parking area.*
Alternative parking at Shillito Wood is signed off the A621 between Owler Bar and Baslow.

The Pub

The Royal Oak at Millthorpe (tel: 0114 289 0870) is an old unspoilt country inn located in the beautiful Cordwell valley. The stone-built pub, reminiscent of an old toll-house, dates from the 17th century. There are two rooms, a cosy nook near to the entrance and another room off to the right of the bar where there are open fires of a winter's night. There are seats outside as well as a beer garden which make this a delightful spot in summer. Ramblers are welcome and the landlord is a keen fell walker too – he points to the many paths in the valley near to the pub!

The cask ales are usually Tetley's Cask Bitter, Marston's Pedigree and Daleside's Old Legover. The Royal Oak is open from 11.30am until 2.30pm, Thursday to Saturday and from 5.30pm (Saturday at 6.00pm) onwards, Tuesdays to Saturdays. It is also open from 12 noon until 3.30pm on Sunday lunchtimes. Please note that the pub is, therefore, not open on Mondays, nor Tuesday and Wednesday lunchtimes nor on Sunday evenings.

Home-made food is served on Thursdays to Sundays from 12 noon until 2.00pm and Friday and Saturday evenings from 6pm until 8.15pm. Families are welcome but as both rooms have bars children under 16 are not allowed inside the pub but many come to enjoy the large garden. Groups of walkers of eight or more are asked to telephone the landlord beforehand.

The Walk

From the Royal Oak, go over the main road and down Mill Lane to the ford. There is a footbridge here for the faint hearted, but the stream is often no more than a trickle. After the ford the road goes right, to a farm, but the right of way goes straight ahead. It is an unusual survival, with parallel routes separated by a hedge. The lower route is a bridleway, well used and often muddy. The upper route is a footpath and usually drier. It was a not uncommon arrangement in packhorse days.

Go through the stile on the right, beyond the entrance to Mill Farm, then keep left by the hedge. Beyond the next stile, bear right, across the field, thus reaching a small bridge. Go over the two stiles and follow the hedge on the left, passing through a gate-cum-stile and now following a hedge on your right. This is a little-walked path and is not obvious underfoot. At the gate by the oak tree, bear left to a very dubious-looking crossing of a stream. There is no bridge and no obvious stepping stones either. Cattle have made the approach rough and muddy so negotiate this as best you may. On the other side go up the bank, bearing left to a gate and thus onto a track. Here you turn right.

Moorhall

The track is a grand example of a green lane – easy walking, but steadily climbing for the most part, sometimes in a sunken hollow-way, other times with glimpses out over the fields. You soon reach the road coming up from the delightfully named Rumbling Street, and so arrive at Moorhall. Turn right, along the lane and follow the road for about a mile, without deviating right or left, until you reach Shillito Wood. When this walk was reconnoitred, the clouds were scudding across the sky, only just above the moor. Rain showers kept obliterating any view

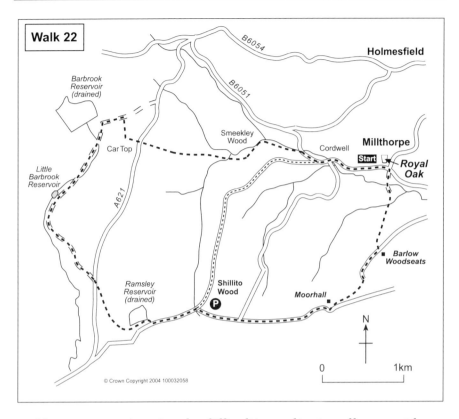

and it was easy to imagine the difficulties earlier travellers must have faced crossing these moors in the absence of any distinguishing features or road signs.

If you are faced with inclement weather and need to get back down to Millthorpe quickly, there is a lane on the right, just before the wood. This takes you rapidly back down to Cordwell Valley.

Medieval Cross

At Shillito Wood turn right, along the waymarked path into the wood to see the fine medieval cross. When you get out of the wood into the car park and onto the road, go left, down to the road junction and bear right. At the junction, there is the stump of another old cross. This is one of several remaining on the Eastern Moors of the Peak District. They were the road signs of their day, vital markers on what were regarded as diffi-cult and dangerous routes. In the 16th and 17th centuries, guides were employed to lead travellers over these moors and – as noted in Walk 14 – the routes were described as "mirey and founderous".

On the left-hand side of the road is Leash Fen, reputedly the site of a market as the old verse describes:

> When Chesterfield was but gorse and broom, then Leash Fen was a market town.
> Now Leash Fen is but gorse and broom and Chesterfield the market town.

Although this seems highly unlikely, historians and archaeologists tell us that these moors were indeed well populated in the Bronze Age, when Chesterfield was part of an uncleared forest.

Continue along the road, which has a wide verge, until you reach a gate on the right, leading onto Ramsley Moor. Go over the stile and enter the National Park's Eastern Moors Estate. Wildlife has been encouraged here since the Park took over, especially in the "sanctuary" areas. Please take heed of the various notices.

Once through the gate, follow the signed path along the base of the former dam. The reservoir has now been drained, apart from some small newly created ponds designed to attract wildlife. Beyond the dam you come onto a wide track with good views over towards Big Moor, Gardom's and Birchen Edges. Soon you round the corner into the upper Barbrook valley. The packhorse routes coming over from Baslow and Curbar can be seen clearly. They descend as deep trenches to cross the Bar Brook just near the crossroads. Far away on the horizon there is the distinctive tuft of trees that marks the top of Minninglow Hill.

Big Moor

The track soon reaches the A621, where there is a stile and gate. Cross the road with care. The road is busy and traffic travels too fast for comfort. Go over the stile opposite and so onto Big Moor. The map marks a number of antiquities on this moor, including field systems, stone circles and enclosures. Numerous Bronze Age relics have been discovered here and it is a salutary thought that humans made their mark on these moors thousands of years ago. The ancient sites are all but swallowed up by encroaching vegetation.

The track follows the line of a culvert, linking the Barbrook reservoirs to Ramsley reservoir. Ownership by the water authorities protected these moors from modern farming practices and when the water companies had no more need of the reservoirs, or the moors, they were handed to the National Park for management. You soon reach Little Barbrook reservoir and shortly afterwards cross the stream on a bridge. There is a surprisingly isolated feel to this walk, despite the fact that the A621 is only about 500m away, but completely hidden.

Keep on up the track towards Big Barbrook reservoir, which, like Ramsley has now been drained and the dam breached. The reservoir keeper's house is still occupied. As you approach this you go over another bridge and then turn right, along the tarmac drive.

In less than 500m, paths cross the drive and there should be a sign-post. Here go right, along a narrow and indistinct path, leaving the metalled lane. The path heads over Car Top and bears left to reach the A621, opposite to a rough lane. Cross the road and go down the lane on an almost dead straight course, towards tree-crowned Smeekley Hill. The view ahead is extensive, right over Chesterfield to the limestone ridge where Bolsover Castle stands defiantly.

Smeekley Farm

Ignoring all turns left or right, carry on downhill, soon passing Smeekley Farm. Just beyond the farm, you go over a bridge and then turn left along a signposted path. This runs beside the stream through delightful mixed woodland. Follow the broadening path by the stream to a crossing of paths and here go straight on, soon leaving the woodland behind. The path crosses the stream on a footbridge, beside a ruined stone bridge. A final section of field path follows and thus you reach the road.

Turn right and follow the road, which has little verge beyond Eweford Bridge, so **take great care**, soon reaching Cordwell Farm. From here on there is a footway that takes you unerringly to the Royal Oak at Millthorpe.

Walk 23. Padley Gorge and Hathersage

The Route: Longshaw car park, Padley Gorge, Upper Padley, Leadmill Bridge, Hathersage, North Lees, Stanage Edge, Burbage Edge, Longshaw.

Distance: 11 miles. Allow 5 hours exclusive of stops.

Start: Longshaw car park (National Trust). (Grid reference 267 802). Public transport users should alight at the Fox House pub, which is nearby.

Maps: OS Explorer OL 1 Dark Peak Area and OL 24 White Peak Area.

How to get there:

By bus – *There is a good daily service to Fox House from Sheffield (buses 272, 274), Buxton (bus 65), Bakewell (bus 240) and Castleton (bus 272). There is a seasonal service from Chesterfield and Dronfield.*

By train – *There is a daily train service to Hathersage and Grindleford stations from Sheffield and Manchester.*

By car – *From Sheffield follow the A625 then A6187 to Fox House then left onto the B6055. The car park is signed about 200 metres from the junction.*
From Chesterfield follow the B6051 to Owler Bar, then the B6054, A625, B6055 almost to the Fox House. Longshaw car park is on the left.
From Bakewell and Buxton directions go to Calver Sough, then A625 to its junction with B6055, then as Chesterfield.

The Pub

The Plough Inn at Leadmill Bridge near Hathersage (tel: 01433 650319) is built on the site of a lead smelting mill, although records indicate that there was probably a corn mill hereabouts before then. However, its fortunes as an alehouse began later when the building was part of a farm known as The Goosetree. By the 19th century, the Plough Inn was established and its fortunes secured as a roadside inn. Its history is captured in the ambience of the hostelry to this day; there are exposed beams, and the woodwork set against brickwork or the original stone. There's a main bar and restaurant with fires in winter to warm the feet.

One of the real joys regarding this inn is its serene setting, nestled as it is on the banks of the River Derwent and the garden, which runs down to the river, is an ideal place to be in summer. Equally, the flowers and hanging baskets, which adorn the inn, make it a welcoming place to stop awhile. The Plough Inn is open from 11.30am every day (12 noon on Sundays) until 11.00pm (10.30pm on Sundays). It serves a range of beers – Theakston's Best Bitter and Old Peculier, and cask beers from Adnams, Batemans, Jennings and Smiles. Food is cooked fresh to order and is available from 11.30am-2.30pm and 6.30-9.30pm on Mondays to Fridays. At weekends, food is served all day from opening until 9.30pm Saturdays and 9.00pm Sundays. Large walking groups need to give notice of their intention to call! Families are welcome but please note that children need to be under control. The Plough Inn offers accommodation, see www.theploughinn-hathersage.com.

The Walk

This is a strenuous walk – *so make certain that you are geared up for it.* Leave the rear of the Longshaw car park by a path signed to the visitor centre. At the junction of paths go right, to the Longshaw Lodge Gate. If coming from the Fox House bus stop, walk to the B6055 junction, cross with care and go through a gate on the far side of the A6187. A path leads down to the Longshaw Lodge Gate. Go through the gate, over the road and over the stile opposite, by another gate. All this land is part of the National Trust's Longshaw Estate and it can get very busy, given its proximity to Sheffield.

Follow the path through the wood, with views to Sir William Hill (with its TV mast) and to the contorted stones of Mother Cap, perched on Millstone Edge. At the fork in the path, keep left, soon reaching a footbridge over the Burbage Brook. Cross the bridge and bear left, alongside the stream.

Padley Gorge

Keep alongside the stream, ignoring paths going off right or left and soon you enter the oak woodland at the start of Padley Gorge. This superb wood is a wonderful survival of the ancient woodland, which once covered much of the Peak District. Its continuation now is a result of careful management, not least being a restriction on the grazing of sheep. For a long time, the moorland sheep were wintered in this wood and they effectively ate any newly seeded trees. This practice has now ceased and the resultant new growth is there for all to see.

The path falls steadily, but the stream descends more rapidly and soon is well below your route. Ignore paths leading up the hillside or down to the stream, keeping right by the part carved millstone. A path joins, coming up from the stream and for a brief moment your path climbs, before resuming its descent. You soon reach the distinctive curved-roof building housing a valve on the great Derwent Aqueduct. This was built in the early years of the 20th century and carries water from the Derwent Dams, down the valley to Derby and other East Midlands towns and cities.

Brunt's Barn

Bear left by the valve house, following the path down to a gate and so into a rough lane. Note what appear to be stone block railway sleepers forming part of the surface of this lane. The lane descends past the houses of Windses Estate to a T-junction. Grindleford station lies just to the left here with trains to Manchester and Sheffield (and a famous café). Ignoring these blandishments, turn right and soon leave the houses behind. The lane soon passes Padley Chapel. This is a reminder of the persecution of local Catholics in earlier times and it is the centre for an annual pilgrimage. On the left is Brunt's barn, the National Park's volunteer centre, named after the late Harry Brunt. He was the Deputy National Park Officer.

Continue along the lane, now no more than a rough track and cross the cattle grid and the remains of a bridge. This carried the lane over a deep cutting, which formed part of the Derwent Valley Water Board's railway. Stone was brought down from Bolehill quarry on this railway and then taken on the Hope Valley line to Bamford, and thence up the water board's branch line to the Derwent and Howden dams.

Pass more houses on the left and go through a gateway. Bear left here, leaving the track and following a sketchy path by the edge of the woodland. Another path is soon joined and you bear left, down through the wood to a gate by the railway bridge. Cross the bridge and go right, through another gate and into Coppice Wood. The path is easily followed but quite rough underfoot. At the bottom of the hill you join the riverside path and bear right, soon reaching open fields.

There follows a delightful riverside walk. After the second stile, the path bears right to Harper Leys, cutting out a loop of the river. waymarks point round the buildings to a kissing gate where you join a lane close to the river. There is a curious collection of carved stones

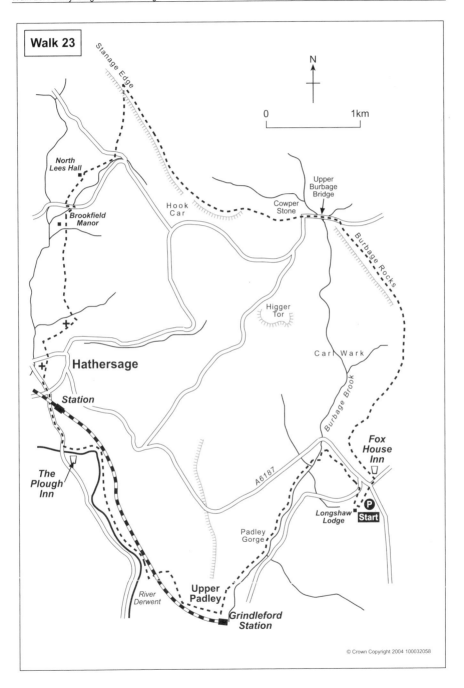

Walk 23

N

0   1km

Stanage Edge

North Lees Hall

Upper Burbage Bridge

Cowper Stone

Hook Car

Brookfield Manor

Burbage Rocks

Higger Tor

Carl Wark

Hathersage

Burbage Brook

Station

Fox House Inn

The Plough Inn

A6187

Longshaw Lodge

Start

Padley Gorge

River Derwent

Upper Padley

Grindleford Station

© Crown Copyright 2004 100032058

here. It looks as if someone had the idea of building a mock Grecian temple, then had second thoughts and abandoned the project.

Follow the lane alongside the river. This is kingfisher and dipper country so keep your eyes wide open. The lane soon runs alongside a mill leat, still carrying water and heralding the approach to Leadmill Bridge. When you reach the main road, the Plough pub lies just to the left, over the bridge.

The route of the walk goes right at the main road. Cross the road onto the footway and go up under the railway bridge (which has no footway). The station approach is on the right – trains to Sheffield and Manchester from here. Buses to Sheffield and Castleton from the stops on the A6187 a bit further on.

Once past the station approach, cross the road and continue ahead until you reach Oddfellows Road, signed to the car park and swimming baths. Turn right here. As you walk along Oddfellows Road, Stanage Edge can be seen away to the left, rising above the roofs of Hathersage. Go past the car park and swimming baths. Where the road swings right, by a green lamp-post, cross over and go down a signposted path. This leads down through a narrow ginnel onto the main road.

Little John's Grave

Cross the road and go along Baulk Lane. Look out for a signpost on the right, pointing the way to the church. The church is clearly in view to your right in any case. Go up the path and enter the churchyard. The church is dedicated to St Michael and All Angels, and the churchyard contains the reputed grave of Little John, Robin Hood's giant lieutenant. It is only fair to say that other less poetical reasons for the large "grave" have been put forward. It is also unfortunate that a large yew bow, which hung in the church until the 19th century, has since vanished.

Go through the churchyard, by the stump of an ancient cross and emerge via the lych gate. These covered gateways were designed to allow coffin bearers to rest, before the final walk into the church. Turn left along the lane. Where the lane bears left, go over a stile, ahead and then turn right. The path forks. Bear left by the ash tree and go steeply down, with some steps for assistance. Descend the field to a stone clapper bridge in the bottom left-hand corner.

From the bridge go straight up the next field and continue climbing until you top the rise. Here the route forks again (signed) and an indistinct path bears right, making for a waymarked stile in the fence. Once over this, continue heading up and across the field to join an old lane near a gateway. This lane was obviously a cart-way from Hathersage at one time. It ran down to the stream you crossed earlier, on a easier gradient to the one you have just used, then turned through a hairpin bend and climbed to meet the path again. Follow the lane, which is no more than a terrace on the hillside. Birchill Wood is on your right and Brookfield manor can be seen below on your left. This is now a conference centre. Cowclose Farm is in view ahead, with North Lees Hall and Stanage Edge beyond.

North Lees Hall

When you reach Cowclose Farm, go through the gate and skirt round to the right of the buildings before gaining the farm access track. This is followed to the road, where you turn left. Almost at once you turn right, leaving the road and going up the driveway to North Lees Hall. The hall is well known for its association with Charlotte Brontë, who used it as the setting for Thornfield Hall in her novel "Jane Eyre". The hall has its own fascinating history. It belonged to the Eyre family, noted Catholics at a time when such religious faith was tantamount to treason. A ruined chapel near the hall was built at the time of James II, whose leanings towards Catholicism cost him his throne. Similar anti-Catholic feeling led to the sacking of the chapel. The hall is now converted into holiday flats.

The path passes the hall and turns sharp right, to a gateway into open fields. Go straight ahead to a stile and gate and so enter the wood. Follow the broad pathway through the wood almost to the road, then go left, up a rough but clear path. This emerges onto the road near the Ranger briefing centre and toilets.

Cross the road and head up the broad green path. Stanage Edge rises impressively to your right and is usually festooned with climbers. The view from here is extensive, to Offerton Hill and round to Mam Tor. The path soon becomes paved, rising steadily through a jumble of boulders to a sheepfold. Beyond this, the path discovers a weakness in the impregnable gritstone wall of Stanage Edge and ascends easily to the crest.

Stanage Edge

Pause here to take in the view, which covers most of the High Peak – Win Hill, Kinder Scout and Bleaklow are all visible. Turn right and follow the edge path; a superb walk along what is arguably the finest gritstone climbing edge in the country. There is no difficulty in route finding here, the path is broad and clear. As you approach Hooks Car the path turns more to the east and avoids the trig point. It is worth visiting the trig point for another spectacular view before returning to the path. Follow the route (paved in places) via Cowper Stone (not the direct route across the moor towards Higger Tor), and so reach the road at Upper Burbage Bridge. For those in need of sustenance, there is often an ice-cream van here in summer.

Cross the two bridges and take the second stile on the right, ignoring the more obvious lower path. Your route is narrow, but clear enough, along the top of Burbage Rocks. Again the view is superb, taking in Carl Wark, an old hillfort site, and Higger Tor. It is worth noting that at this point you are in the city of Sheffield. Not many cities can boast such scenery.

Eventually the path tends downwards through tumbled boulders. The route swings left at a stream and climbs steadily. At a point marked by three cairns, there is a crossing of paths. Go straight on, but soon bear right and regain the crest of the rocks. There are some dramatic rock faces on this stretch, the work of early quarrymen. At the biggest of these, there are several millstones in various stages of completion that were abandoned when the quarry closed. The overhangs here are spectacular, but the edges are loose – *so keep away*.

Longshaw

Now you will see ahead to Longshaw Pond and the main road leading to Surprise View. The path descends past an abandoned, part hollowed-out stone trough, cracked right through. Imagine your annoyance at getting to this stage, only to find all your work was wasted. At the crossing of paths, bear left and follow a narrow path to emerge onto the A6187 road just before the Fox House. (If you are heading for Longshaw car park, cross the road and go into Longshaw Estate, retracing your steps. Longshaw Lodge has a fine information display and sells food and drinks (to 5.00pm), essentials after a ramble of this length. If you want the pub instead, The Fox House Inn, evidently named after a Mr Fox, a path leads off left just before you reach the road and this lands you fairly and squarely in the pub car park. There are bus stops here for the return journey.

Walk 24. Rainow

The Route: The Robin Hood Inn, Common Barn, Waggonshaw Brow, Saddle Cote, Harrop Fold Farm, Billinge Head Farm, Smithy Lane.

Distance: 5 miles. Allow 2½ hours exclusive of stops.

Start: The Robin Hood Inn, Smithy Lane, Rainow. There is a small amount of roadside parking available in the village but please park with consideration to residents.

Map: OS Explorer OL 24 – The Peak District, White Peak Area.

How to get there:

By bus – *Daily service, buses 60-64 from Macclesfield, Whaley Bridge and New Mills plus an extra Sunday morning journey, 57 bus, from Whaley Bridge.*

By car – *From Macclesfield or Whaley Bridge, travel on the B5470 to Rainow village.*

The Pub

The Robin Hood Inn at Rainow (tel: 01625 574060) is located at the top of the village between the church and what was at one time a chapel at an appropriately named spot, Chapel Brow. The inn is situated in fine walking country and is a little more than half a mile from the Gritstone Trail, so is handy for those looking for an overnight stop on this route. The pub is a popular village local but is also frequented by ramblers calling in before or after their walk. The Robin Hood is divided into a number of areas including a small dining area, a cosy middle bar and a larger room to the right of the bar extending to the darts and pool table area. There's a convivial atmosphere and the landlord is a keen supporter of the rural community. There are seats outside the front of the house and beyond the car park.

The pub is open from 12 noon onwards every day. Cask ales include, Black Sheep Best Bitter, Greenall's Bitter and an ever-changing guest beer. Food is served from 12 noon until 2.00pm every day, from 6.45pm until 8.45pm on Wednesdays to Saturdays and 12 noon until 5.00pm on Sundays. Families are welcome but please note that there is not a separate children's menu. Overnight accommodation is also available.

Rainow village

The Walk

From the Robin Hood Inn (main road entrance) turn left to walk along the pavement towards the cluster of houses which surround Gin Clough mill. However, before approaching a group of houses on the left, cross over the main road to walk up a track. It is signposted as a path and there is also a sign for Slack-oth-Moor farm. This rises relentlessly to the shoulder of the hillside, passing turns to farmsteads on your left. It begins to dip, crosses a cattle grid and then levels in a large field. As the track bears right, keep ahead in order to cross a stone step-stile in the left-hand corner. Do not go left over a stile here – keep straight on. Continue ahead in a similar direction towards a large farm known as Common Barn. Cross a stile, walk through the yard between barns and on reaching the drive cross this too. Keep ahead over two stiles to enter a field.

Waggonshaw Brow

Once in the field, proceed ahead, with the wall to your left and again step over another stile into rougher ground. Your way is very slightly left as the path rises and curves to a stile – there is a guide marker. Once over the stile, follow the green path as it curves down Waggonshaw Brow; the name suggests that this was an old wagon way, possibly for carrying salt from Cheshire to eastern towns. The views across Lamaload reservoir and to Shutlingsloe hill are impressive from here.

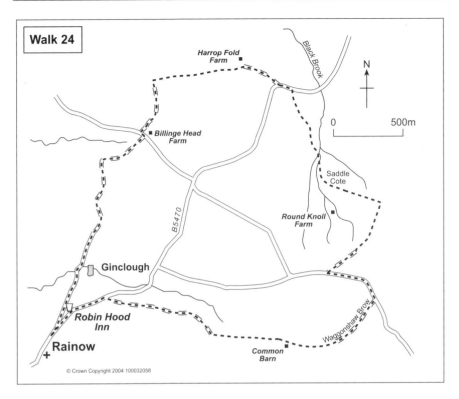

You come near to an old farmstead. The path deviates to the left and skirts the rear of this building then drops down to a barred gate where there's also a stile to cross. Keep left to walk up the drive to a stile, which exits onto the road. Go left and follow this as it bends and descends towards Blue Boar Farm, which was also a public house long ago. Before reaching the buildings, go right along a narrow metalled road, Bank Lane, This becomes a rougher track and within 100 metres look for a stile on the left which enters a field. Now, bear right across a rough patch at first, then bear slightly left to follow the head of the ridge to a stile. Cross it.

Saddle Cote

This is actually a meeting point with a cross path. Go left and cross another stile into a large field. The views across to Charles Head on the right and the Harrop Valley below are exceptional from this isolated spot known as Saddle Cote. Keep company with the dry-stone wall to the left as you descend the hillside. As you come closer to the little wooded clough below bear slightly right and the path leads into the clough where you will encounter wet ground and a small stream, the Moss Brook, to traverse. Go over the stile and rise up to your left over an even smaller tributary and then the path runs parallel to the fence and the remains of a dry-stone wall. The wall then curves left to a rather wet field corner and as this tapers you will notice two stiles. Go over the one on the right as it is the drier route to the main B5470 road.

Once in the next field, head slightly left. You are walking almost parallel to the field wall and a track and farm buildings seen above on your left. Keep ahead and, for the few final metres of the field, the path dips to a stile and signpost. Cross the stile and the road. Go left to walk facing the traffic for a few moments until you reach the corner.

Harrop Fold Farm

Climb the stile and make a beeline for the stile opposite. This brings you to a drive, ahead, which leads down to Harrop Fold Farm. This begins to bend right towards the farm. At this point, go left over a ladder stile and then bear immediately right over a stone step-stile. Descend to a coral behind a barn, and after it drop again, left, to cross a stile. Now bear right to walk down the field but be on the lookout for a stile by a gate in a dip. It sits between hawthorns. Cross it and keep ahead to reach the next stile, which is beneath holly bushes.

It may now feel as if you are completely lost, and, once again, you might decide to deride or even curse the authors. Bear with us for there is a way through. In this enclosure, best described as a thicket, the path bends to the right at first and then to the left to pass over a wooden footbridge. However, even more attention is now required. In the next field rise up the bank and then continue straight ahead across rough ground. Keep to the left of a gully and, after a few steps more, you should spot the stile hidden beneath a rather exuberant holly bush. Cross the stile and footbridge. Walk triumphantly ahead towards a landmark, which this time is the roof of a dwelling. The path exits at the next field boundary onto a lane.

Billinge Head Farm

Go left to pass the dwelling and walk up the lane to a road where Billinge Head Farm stands to your left. Be careful here as some drivers travel too fast for the poor road conditions on this road. Go left, cross over just before the farm to enter a rough track in the direction of the hamlet of Rainowlow.

However, at the fork make sure that you keep left. This climbs beneath Big Low and you pass a few dwellings on this section. The track begins to descend to pass Back-of-the-Crofts farm on the right. It then drops to a junction. Keep ahead here to walk into Rainow. There are a number of good viewpoints along this section and as if by chance you arrive back at the Robin Hood and the bus shelter, a very traditional one, for the bus to Macclesfield. Check the timetable as some pass by on the other side of the road! Perhaps, it would be better to call into the pub while you are thinking about where to stand.

Walk 25. Rivelin

The Route: Rivelin Mill car park, The Lawns, Moorwood Lane , Ronksley Hall Farm, The New Norfolk, Wyming Brook, Fox Holes, Blackbrook, Coppice Wood.

Distance: 5 miles. Allow 3 hours exclusive of stops.

Start: Rivelin Mill Car Park (Grid Reference 291873).

Map: OS Explorer OL 1 – The Peak District, Dark Peak Area.

How to get there:

By bus – *Daily service from Sheffield and Castleton, 273 and 274, which set down near to the car park, as does the RuralLinks service 64 from Hillsborough Interchange.*

By car – *The car park is signed from the A57 Manchester Road if approaching from the West or Sheffield City Centre. Travel on the A6101 Rivelin Valley Road if approaching from the M1 Motorway or Sheffield's northern suburbs.*

The Pub

The Sportsman (tel: 0114 230 1935) on Redmires Road is one of eleven similarly named pubs in Sheffield but this is the only one which is home to a kite flying club and you can see why. The pub is fronted by a wide bay window and there's a great view across the Rivelin Valley toward Sheffield. To the left is a large field where there are a small number of seats. The Sportsman almost certainly served the purpose of slaking the thirst of the workers involved in building the Redmires reservoirs and in later years, those stationed at a nearby military camp. Nowadays, it welcomes locals and visitors to the area in equal measure.

The Sportsman is open at lunchtime usually from 11.30am to 3.30pm and from 5.00pm in the evenings. Food is served from noon and from 6.00-8.00pm. However, on Sundays it is from 12 noon until 4.00pm. The pub is usually open all day at weekends. Hand-pulled beers include Stones Bitter and Timothy Taylor's Landlord.

The Walk

For the most part, the first part offers an easy ramble but it gets tougher on the return leg. Leave the car park by the solitary car access and cross

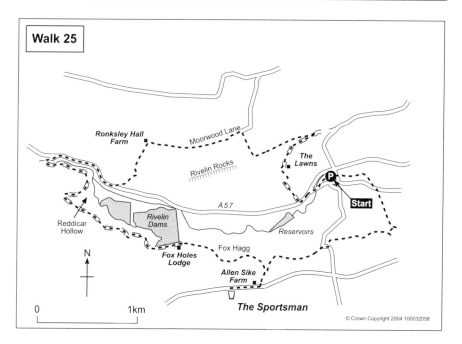

Walk 25

Ronksley Hall Farm
Moorwood Lane
The Lawns
Rivelin Rocks
A57
Start
Reddicar Hollow
Rivelin Dams
Reservoirs
N
Fox Holes Lodge
Fox Hagg
Allen Sike Farm
0   1km   *The Sportsman*
© Crown Copyright 2004 100032058

the road to the signboard. The bus stops within 5 minutes walk of this point so is very handy. This interpretation explains the Rivelin Valley Nature Trail and there is also some information about the past industrial history. All of the mills that were once housed here are gone, but many of the dams remain, havens for wildlife and popular recreational spots for the residents of Sheffield.

Return to the car park and walk through it onto what was obviously a dam wall. The Rivelin Brook is to the left and a silted mill-pond to the right. At the bridge, which happens to be a fine example of turnpike road architecture, go right along the A57 for a short distance. Pass by the post office and toilets. Cross the wide mouth of the Rivelin Valley Road with care then, at the footpath sign, go right, through a white gate and ascend the track to Lawns Farm.

On entering the farm compound, go left through the yard then right up the hill. The route is shown as a track but it rapidly deteriorates to a narrow path. This can get muddy and overgrown so a stick comes in handy – and wearing shorts would amount to sheer masochism. The wall, to your right is a sure guide. At the waymark, continue by the wall and mercifully, the path leads onto Woodbank Road, which is only a narrow lane.

Bingley Seat

On Woodbank Road go left to pass Bingley Seat which affords views across the valley. The lane begins to climb with rock outcropping to the right. Follow the lane as it bears sharp right. This levels and reaches a T-junction. Go left here and pass by another seat, which offers good views across the moors high above Sheffield.

Moorwood Lane

At the next junction, keep left and then the track kinks to the right and ahead again. This is Moorwood Lane and the large farm seen across the fields to your right is Moorwood Farm. The views up the valley are grand with Derwent Edge on the skyline. The track continues to Ronkesley Hall Farm, a fine Jacobean style building in a commanding position.

At Ronksley Hall Farm, go left to walk down the hill on Onksley Lane which soon becomes metalled. This descends more steeply and swings right as it cuts the line of Rivelin Rocks. It then continues to run down to the A57 road. Cross the main road to the footway and, if you require refreshment, turn left for the New Norfolk. If not, go right to walk along the pavement for approximately one quarter of a mile to a lay-by known as Hollow Meadows. Here you go down a track to leave the A57 behind, thankfully.

Rivelin Dam

Follow the main trail over the bridge and Wyming Brook. The path is easy to follow as it curves around Reddicar Clough and rises through woodland to Millstone Hole. Here, you reach a major junction. Follow the lower track as it descends towards the reservoir. Ignore any tempting paths off to the right; simply keep to the main track until you reach Fox Holes Lodge and the Rivelin Dam. The views across the water are particular good from this vantage point.

As the road bends left to run over the dam, you go through a gap-stile on the right by the gate and then go right onto the second waymarked path rising away from the car park area. The path begins to climb the hillside. Keep right at the junctions to ensure that you walk up to Allen Sike, a deep clough – *so please take care*. You come to a three-fingered post. For the Sportman's pub, it is necessary to deviate to the right just beyond the signpost. This leads up to Redmires Road and the pub is to the right. Retrace your steps afterwards (or there is a 51 bus from here to

Rivelin reservoir

Sheffield Interchange for those who want to cut the walk short). Otherwise, keep left at the signpost, and this path bends to the left and runs along the side of the clough. Ignore paths to the right but progress ahead on this path, which rises gradually up the hillside. Your path rises up to a junction with Lodge Lane. There are great views from here back up the valley.

Black Brook

Cross over and walk up the road for a few metres before cutting left. This well-used path cuts along the top of the valley with a wall and fence to the right. There's a golf course on other side. It then plummets down the Black Brook clough to cross a little stream via a series of stones and rises out of the valley again with a wall or fence on your right. Pass by a step-stile in the wall and not long beyond, you reach a junction of paths. The one ahead which keeps company with a wall is not the way. At this junction, you need to go left to descend through the wood but be sure not to take a lesser path cutting left again at this point. Your path gradually descends and runs more or less ahead or slightly right at this stage. However, it soon becomes less determinate and bends left to approach a wall and open enclosures. Do not cross the wall to enter the pastures. The path heads left of the wall at this point and runs through the wood above the enclosures and then bends right to follow a piece of wall which runs down to a track known as Coppice

Road. There are a number of trodden paths in this wood so it can be a little confusing. The key is to ensure that you descend by the wall adjacent to the three strips of narrow fields.

This gives out onto a track, Coppice Road, where you bear left for the hop, skip and jump to the A57. Bus stops for the 273/274 buses to Castleton (this side) and for Sheffield across the road are located to the right. Otherwise, cross the road, and walk left until you see a bridleway on the right. Follow this back to the riverside and cross the bridge back to the car park. The bus stop for the bus to Hillsborough Interchange is just to the right at the crossroads on the A6101.

Walk 26. Robin Hood (near Baslow)

The Route: Robin Hood, Gardom's Edge, Jack Flat, Wellington's monument, Eagle Stone, Clod Hall X roads, Nelson's Monument, Birchen Edge, Robin Hood.

Distance: 4 miles. Allow 2 hours exclusive of stops.

Start: Robin Hood pub. The public car park is adjacent to the pub. It gets very busy at weekends and space could be at a premium. (Grid reference 280 721).

Map: OS Explorer OL 24 – The Peak District, White Peak Area.

How to get there:

By bus –   *There are daily services from Chesterfield, Bakewell,(170) Manchester, Stockport (X67) and Buxton (66) to the Robin Hood Inn.*

               There is also a daily service from Sheffield, Buxton, Leek and the Potteries which calls at Clod Hall crossroads, approximately 1 mile away).

By car –   *From Chesterfield follow the A619 (signed to Chatsworth and Buxton) to the Robin Hood.*

               From Sheffield follow the A621 to the junction with the A619, then left, on the A619 to the Robin Hood.

               From Bakewell follow the A619, through Baslow towards Chesterfield to the Robin Hood.

The Pub

The Robin Hood Inn near Baslow (tel: 01246 583186) is very well known among the rambling and climbing worlds, nestling as it does, at the foot of Birchen Edge. This long-standing roadside inn is, fortunately, on the old road set back from the very busy A619. You may catch sight of the name of a previous landlord, a Mr Ollivant, on a lintel above the left-hand entrance. Therein lies a tale. An extract from a local rag "This Week" dating from 20th July, 1889 chronicles an amusing tale:

"At Bakewell on Saturday, before Mr R.W.M. Nesfield, Catherine Stevenson, of Nottingham, in custody, was charged with breaking several panes of glass in the window of The Robin Hood public house near Baslow, on the previous night. A man, said to be her husband tried

The Robin Hood

to prevent Mr Ollivant the landlord, from securing the woman. With assistance, he put both into an outbuilding and kept them there until the police arrived. Both were then conveyed to the Bakewell lock-up. The woman had torn one of the legs off the man's trousers whilst in the outbuilding. He was discharged and the woman sent to prison for four-teen days."

There is a walkers' den (non-carpeted area) where boots and dogs are welcome. The Robin Hood serves Mansfield Cask Ale and Riding Bitter, Banks's Bitter and Marston's Pedigree on hand-pull. The inn is open all day during the summer except on Mondays when the hours are from 11.30am until 3pm and from 6.30pm onwards. In winter, the inn is open at these hours on other days except Sunday when it is open from 12 noon until 4pm and from 6.30pm until 10.30pm. In the summer food is served all day and during winter from 11.30am until 2.30pm and from 6.30pm until 8pm in the evening. There is also accommodation available at the inn and families are welcome.

The Walk

From the Robin Hood, go down the road to the junction with the A619. Follow the A619 towards Baslow for a short distance, and then go right, over a stile. The path soon crosses a terrace, which marks the line of the old Chesterfield road, which was turnpiked in 1758. It was superseded by the present A619 in the late 18th century and a toll house was erected at The Robin Hood.

The path climbs gently onto rough pasture land. According to the map there were "ancient enclosures" here, but it takes a well trained eye to distinguish these now. The East Moors of the Peak District were settled in the Bronze Age and the inhabitants left a wealth of artefacts for the archaeologist to discover.

The path tops the rise, giving a view towards Birchen Edge (right) and the Nelson Monument. To the left, the land plunges steeply to the Barbrook valley, with a view into the central Peak, Eaglestone Flat and the Wellington Monument.

Follow the broad path, passing to the left of the pile of rocks and soon begin the descent to Barbrook. The path soon becomes embroiled in scrubby birch woodland below Gardom's Edge, but it is easy enough underfoot and obvious on the ground. A pleasant stroll takes you steadily down to a stile and thus onto the main A621 road.

Wellington's Monument

Cross the road, with care, and go down the unsigned path opposite. The path descends to cross the Bar Brook. Note the houses on the right, spectacularly situated above the river. You now begin the ascent to Wellington's Monument. The path rises steeply, through scrubby woodland; an area known as Jack Flat – a classic bit of Derbyshire understatement.

Just below the tumbled rocks on which the monument stands, the path veers left, following a wall. There are various direct routes of ascent, but it is easier to keep along the clear path until it meets the main route coming up from Baslow. Here you turn sharp right and follow the Bar Road, which is no more than a rough track, up onto the top of the moor. The monument lies just to the right. It was built to commemorate Wellington's victory over Napoleon at Waterloo in 1815. It is a grand viewpoint, overlooking Barbrook, Chatsworth, Gardom's and Birchen Edges. It is also a good place for a rest!

Discretion is the better part of valour

Just across the moor from the monument lies the Eagle Stone. It is an unprepossessing lump of rock, looking for all the world like cowpats piled on top of one another. However, local folklore has it that no man was allowed to wed a Baslow girl until he had climbed the Eagle Stone. It cries out to be climbed, so make your way across the moor to it. As you approach, what seemed to be a simple climb, gradually assumes a different aspect. There is a singular lack of good hand and footholds and the ledges around the Stone all seem to slope outwards. The authors can also say, with confidence, that it is one of those rocks that looks twice as high when you are on top of it than it seemed when you were on the ground. Having decided that you don't want to wed a Baslow girl in any case, you can retreat unashamed, back to the Wellington monument, and then go left along the Bar Road, passing a recently erected guide stone. The track swiftly carries you down to the Curbar Gap road, close to Clod Hall crossroads.

Bar Road

The Bar Road used to be the main road from Sheffield to Baslow until 1808 when the present A621 was built. In the Peak District, most of the present-day main roads came into existence in the 75 years between 1750 and 1825. Some were on the alignment of earlier packhorse routes, but many were entirely new. There has never been such a spate of road building since, despite changes in road transport technology.

Onto Birchen Edge

Turn right at the road and go down to the crossroads, crossing the Barbrook again in the process (buses from Sheffield and the Potteries stop here). Go over the crossroads and then immediately right, over a stile and back onto moorland again. The path strikes out almost due south, heading for the northern end of Birchen Edge. Other paths deviate right towards Gardom's Edge, but ignore these. Continue gently upwards, through scattered birch trees until you are almost level with the rocks. Here the path forks, almost imperceptibly. The main (easy) path goes straight on, along the base of the Edge. The left-hand path scrambles up through the rocks to reach the trig point on the summit. Go on, be a devil, take the left-hand path. (If you miss this, there are other opportunities further on which allow you to access the top of the edge, without the need for rope and tackle). The trig point is another grand viewpoint and a reason for a breather.

"England Expects"

Go along the Edge towards Nelson's Monument, which commemorates the Battle of Trafalgar. To reinforce the nautical flavour, the three prominent rocks on top of the edge are called the "Three Ships" and are inscribed with the names of ships of Nelson's fleet. Many of the climbs

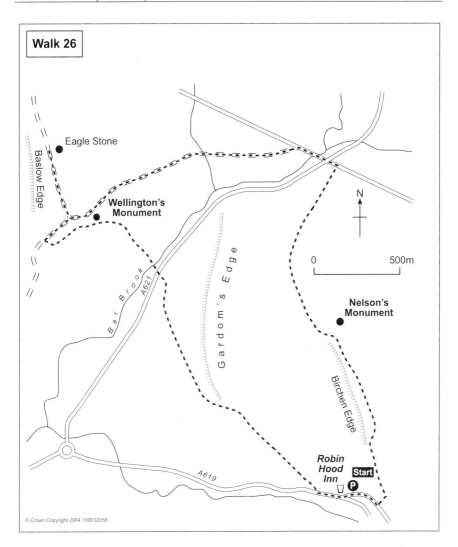

on the Edge also have nautical associations, such as the "Powder Monkey Traverse".

Proceed along the edge until the path suddenly dips, by a set of stop valves. Here turn sharp right and go down a very rough little gully *(care needed here)* to rejoin the main path below the edge. Go left, and romp down the remaining length of the path to reach the road just above the Robin Hood pub and the car park.

Walk 27. Rushton Spencer and Danebridge (Wincle)

The Route: Barleigh Ford Bridge, Wincle Grange, Danebridge, Hammond's Hole, Dane Valley conduit, Rushton Spencer.

Distance: 7 to 8 miles. Allow 4 hours exclusive of stops.

Start: The Knot Inn, Station Road (Grid reference 936 625).

Map: OS Explorer OL 24 – The Peak District, White Peak Area.

How to get there:

By bus – *There is a daily service, bus 107 from Macclesfield to Leek and Derby. Ask for Station Road, Rushton Spencer. The Knot Inn is on the left-hand side of Station Road.*

By car – *From Leek or Macclesfield, travel on the A523 to the village of Rushton Spencer. Turn into Station Road (on your right from the Macclesfield direction), pass the Knot Inn and turn left before the old railway station house. There is a small car park here.*

The Pub

The Ship at Wincle (tel: 01260 227217) is a firm favourite with those who enjoy good food, and a beer that is invariably in excellent condition. There are two bars; a lounge to the right and a flag stoned walker's bar to the left that makes it a firm favourite with many local ramblers. There is also a seating area to the rear of the pub, which is an ideal retreat on a summer's evening.

The Ship Inn certainly dates back several centuries and would have been well located on the old road to Leek. By all accounts, the rebellious Scottish army, led by Bonnie Prince Charlie, called in sometime during 1745. At least one account refers to the way in which the sadly depleted group of soldiers had to leave in haste; evidently the departure was so hasty that one of the soldiers left a gun and a piece of a newspaper dating from the time.

The pub is situated half way along the walk and perhaps more importantly, can be enjoyed after the harder section has been completed. Thus, it offers a welcome break at a lovely spot in this deservedly popular walking area. It is open lunchtimes and evenings

The Ship at Wincle

during the week and all day at weekends except Monday when the inn is closed. There is a changing range of cask beers available. Families are welcome.

The Walk

From the entrance to the Knot Inn, go left on Station Road and opposite the old railway station house, dating from 1844, bear right through a gap-stile to join the old railway track-bed. This was once part of the much loved Knotty line from North Rode junction to Leekbrook junction and then onwards down the Churnet Valley. For decades, the railway brought many visitors to this impressive rural station from The Potteries and Maccles-field. The 1908 'Official guide to the district adjacent to the North Staffordshire Railway', describes Rushton Spencer on page 139 as 'an extensive parish... The houses are scattered and the chief interest is centred in the beautiful valley of scenery of the Dane Valley and the surrounding neighbourhood '.

Fortunately, this remains true nearly 100 years later, for development and even modern farming methods have not altered the landscape significantly. The old track-bed links one long-distance walk, The Staffordshire Way to another, The Gritstone Trail, near to the county boundary between Staffordshire and Cheshire. Both trails offer exceptionally good walking from Rushton Spencer.

Follow the track-bed until it comes to an over bridge where walkers are requested to descend to the left down the embankment to cross a stile. The Gritstone Trail extension to Bosley Cloud and Mow Cop lies ahead but, on this occasion, you need to cut to the right under the bridge and then walk ahead to a stile, which leads to the main A523 road. The route of this ramble follows The Gritstone Trail as far as Dumkins Cross and there are Gritstone markers en route to assist your navigation.

Cross the main road with extreme care and make your way over the stile to enter pastureland. Walk along the crescent-shaped ridge to the next boundary where another stile is crossed. Head slightly right up the field to join the canal feeder where it is crossed by a stone bridge. Go left here along the well-worn path adjacent to the canal feeder, which channels water from the Rive Dane to Rudyard Lake and the Caldon and Trent and Mersey canal network. Proceed along the path to an exit point where a road crosses the canal. Here, go left on the road to descend into the Dane Valley as waymarked with The Gritstone Trail logo.

Barleigh Ford Bridge

The bridge across the river affords fine views of this beautiful stretch of water, rich in wildlife and the bird life is evident to anyone willing to spare a few moments to watch the river banks. At the next corner, as the road rises and bends to the right, keep ahead to cross a stile and then head slightly right to rise up the wooded hillside to pasture. Keep ahead through this pastureland, which is parallel to a wooded clough, seen to your left. The ground becomes wetter as you proceed ahead, guided by the occasional waymark post. You hit another wet area by a cluster of trees and the path rises slightly right out of the valley to meet an old greenway, running in a similar direction on slightly higher ground.

Go left along the greenway to cross a stile by a gate. Keep ahead and you will pass a stile on the right for Whitelee. The waymarked path follows a tree-lined sunken lane, which was most probably one of the major routes to Wincle Grange, trodden by monks and traders several centuries ago. This is the point where you leave The Gritstone Trail to continue ahead over a stile to rise on this delightful old way. Follow the line to two barred gates. Cross a stile here and climb the bank ahead. Keep company with a wall to your right and then the path curves down to pass through wet ground. Cross a stile and proceed up the field.

Wincle Grange

On your left is Wincle Grange, a splendid stone dwelling once a farming settlement associated with Combermere Abbey in the south of Cheshire. The medieval monastic orders were substantial landowners and their farming outposts almost invariably included isolated settlements where contemplation and cultivation were the order of the day. Cross a stile to join a metalled road. Go right here and pass by a small pool to the right, no doubt a popular location for the heron. The road bends to the left and begins to dip. Look for step-stile, some 20 metres ahead, and cross this to enter a field. Head slightly left towards the

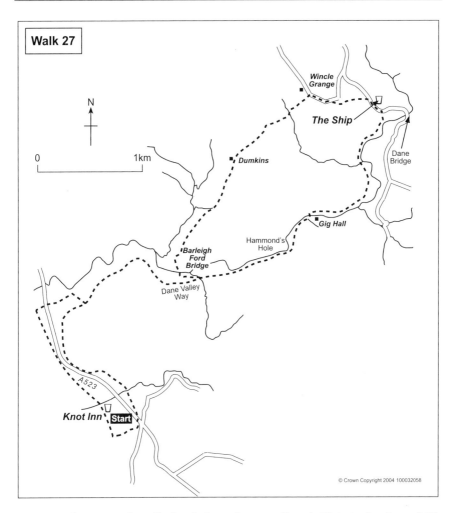

Walk 27

N

0   1km

Wincle Grange

The Ship

Dumkins

Dane Bridge

Gig Hall

Hammond's Hole

Barleigh Ford Bridge

Dane Valley Way

Knot Inn Start

A523

© Crown Copyright 2004 100032058

canopy of trees and a stile leads into the woodland. This is the downhill run to the pub so you are entitled to gather speed. Cross the next stile and head down a field to yet another stile leading into a drive. Cross the stiles and drive to proceed ahead in the next field. This leads to the road at Danebridge. Go right.

Danebridge

You soon arrive at The Ship and after refreshment, no doubt, you will be pleased to read that part two of the walk is less exacting. Whilst it offers more than a saunter along the banks of the Dane, the walk is located in the valley bottom and hence fairly level. From the Ship Inn, go left along the road to the Dane Bridge. Just before the bridge, go right along a track, as signposted, to pass the fisheries and Pringle Cottage. At the cottage, you slip to the left along a cordoned section, which runs near to the Dane; it is a surfaced path at this point. This gives out and the temptation is to stay alongside the river but in the next pasture, the path follows a line beneath the wooded bluff to your right.

The path is fairly clear on the ground and you will notice the occasional waymark, indicating that this is the Dane Valley Way, which follows the course of the river from its gathering grounds at Axe Edge to the Cheshire plains. Cross a stile at the end of the field and continue ahead, nearer to the river until you reach a footbridge. As you cross the bridge, pause awhile to catch glimpses of the beauty of the river as it tumbles over the weir. Ahead is Gig Hall but your way is to the right on a wide path adjacent to the conduit. It is straightforward. Firstly, you pass a building to your right and then the way becomes more akin to a track leading to the road and bridge where you peeled off on the outward section of the walk. Now continue along it back to the village of Rushton Spencer.

Rushton Spencer

Follow the path that sits alongside the conduit into the village. Pass by the Rushton Inn (please note there's no access to the pub at this point) and onwards, passing over a series of stiles and lanes until the conduit reaches the main A523 road. At all times the path follows the feeder canal. It is clear on the ground but there are several stiles to cross and a few tracks too. The walker is asked to pass by with consideration, however, as the conduit follows a line adjacent to gardens and near to dwellings.

At the main road, you will note the Royal Oak pub to your left and the bus stops to the right. Cross over and enter the field on the opposite side. A well worn-path runs left, parallel to the conduit for about 30 metres, and then cuts right across the field to an ornate gate. Continue to the bridge over the old railway line. At the bridge, go over the stile on the left, then drop down to the track. Bear right for the last short section to the Knot Inn.

Walk 28. Walker Barn

The Route: Walker Barn, Ashtreetop, Macclesfield Forest, The Leather Smithy, Langley, The Hollins, Macclesfield Canal.

Distance: 6 miles. Allow 3 hours exclusive of stops.

Start: The Old Setter Dog, Walker Barn (Grid reference 956 737).

Map: OS Explorer OL 24 – The Peak District, White Peak Area.

How to get there:

By bus – *There is a daily service, 58, between Buxton and Macclesfield. Ask for Walker Barn. The one-time public house, the Setter Dog, is now a dwelling on the left-hand side of the road in the direction of Buxton, opposite the junction with the old Buxton road to Tegg's Nose.*

By car – *From Buxton or Macclesfield, travel on the A537 road to Walker Barn. Be warned: there is no car park in the hamlet of Walker Barn and the road is dangerous here too. There is, however, a lay-by before reaching Walker Barn when coming from Buxton after the bend and junction at Turnshawflat. It is a short walk along the verge to the start of the walk. However, you are advised to park in Macclesfield or Buxton and catch the bus for this linear walk!*

The Pubs

There are several pubs to mention on this route so you are likely to find one to suit your taste. The first is the Leather Smithy, overlooking Ridgegate Reservoir. It has two bars, a lounge and a bar with flagstones and this suits most ramblers. There is also a seating area outside at the rear of the pub. A range of real ales is on offer and the pub has a long-standing reputation for food. The second pub is the St Dunstan Inn, a friendly public house in Langley village, which serves Banks bitter and Marston's bitter and a guest beer. It is not usually open on weekday lunchtimes but certainly welcomes walkers in the evening and at weekends.

The last two pubs on the list are situated on the last urban stretch of the walk in Macclesfield and both have been featured in the CAMRA Good Beer Guide in recent years. The Dolphin Inn is situated on Windmill Street, a traditional and homely Robinson's pub which sells a range of beers from the Stockport brewery. It is open 12-2.30pm and from 5.30pm onwards during the week and all day on Saturdays and Sundays. Home-cooked food is served at lunchtimes with the exception of Sunday. Finally, the walk finishes in Waters Green, near the railway and bus stations. Between the two you will find the Waters Green Tavern, which has a deservedly excellent reputation for serving fine ales. It attracts a wide range of clientele from campanologists to the local cycling group, as well as walkers returning from the hills at early doors. The Waters Green Tavern is open from 11.30am-3.00pm and from 5.30pm onwards each day except weekends when the evening opening is at 7.00pm.

The Walk

This walk is not difficult but there are one or two steep climbs in the early stages and a descent of a clough which requires steady footwork; otherwise it is not demanding. The bus usually stops just before the old Setter Dog or on the junction with the old Buxton Road on the way out of Macclesfield. From Buxton, it is likely to stop at the opposite side of the road. Assuming that you have come from Macclesfield, walk on the pavement as it narrows to squeeze past the old inn dating from 1740 according to the tablet above the door. The closure was a sad loss to this isolated community some 260 years later. Pass by a cottage next door and then take care to cross the road in order to walk down the lane on the right known as Crooked Yard Road.

You will see Lower Windyway Farm on the left. Go left over a ladder stile situated opposite a barn here. In the field bear slightly right and the path passes to the left of a stone water trough and climbs up the field to another stile which you cross. There are some exceptional views across to Tegg's Nose Country Park and the upper Bollin Valley from here. Make your way towards the drive to Warrilowhead Farm and take a path parallel to it in the direction of the gateway to the farm. Be sure to keep to the path which is to the right of the gateway; there's a stone step-stile here which you cross. The path skirts beneath the garden, passing by two stone troughs and hitting a patch of wet ground, presumably a spring and hence the reason for the farm location on the spring line at this point.

Keep ahead as best as you can to ascend to the field corner where you cross a stone step-stile. The next section involves a steep descent

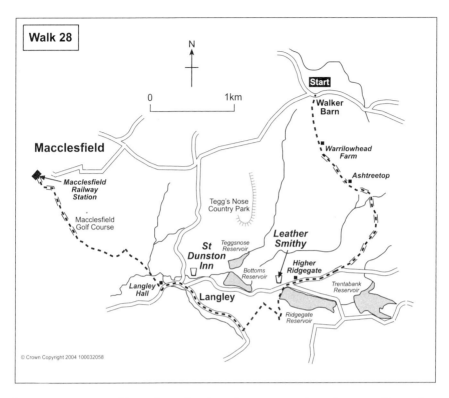

between gorse and hawthorn bushes; it can sometimes be wet. Cross the stream, climb up to a dry-stone wall and proceed ahead with a dry-stone wall to your right. As you approach the dwelling, Ashtreetop, cross the stile and walk ahead through a small plantation. You pass to the right of the dwelling to exit onto a road at a stile.

Macclesfield Forest

At the road bear left and then almost immediately right to enter Macclesfield Forest, at one time a royal hunting ground and now a major tract of coniferous forestry with spruce, pine and larch in ascendancy. There has been an increasing amount of deciduous woodland planted in recent times and the foresters have designed more routes for recreational access. Your path leads down to another track where you bear left; this leads up to an old barn known as Dimples. There is a meeting of tracks here and you take the lower route and turn right to descend through the woodland. Continue down the hillside until you reach a metalled road. You might meet mountain bikers on this section as it is a shared track.

On the road, go right to walk down to The Leather Smithy public house, which sits at a junction and overlooks the impressive Ridgegate reservoir. Gone are the days when we take water for granted and this gathering ground serves the Macclesfield area well. A few paces beyond the pub and opposite a cottage, there is a stile on the left. Cross this and walk ahead along the track that runs parallel to the reservoir retaining wall. At the entrance to the wood, turn right and dip down to a stream, which is crossed by way of a footbridge. Go over the stile in the dry-stone wall, climb up to the track and turn right.

This is the Gritstone Trail but you are not on it for long. As you approach the waterworks look for a well-hidden stile on the left beneath a canopy of trees. Keep ahead to rise up the field to join a hedgerow. Cross a stile and walk ahead towards a dwelling. Cross a small foot-bridge and proceed ahead to join a concrete drive where there's a stile. Walk ahead to the road at a point where the footpath sign is located. Turn right to walk along this quiet road, Cock Hall Lane, into Langley village.

Langley

The road leads to the bus stop and shelter where buses to Macclesfield depart so this is a potential cut off point (buses run until after 10.00pm on Mondays to Saturdays). Pass by the Methodist chapel and at the junction go left unless you happen to make the one-minute detour to the St Dunstan's public house situated amid a long terrace on the High Street.

Otherwise, continue ahead to walk by the old works on the left, the village hall on the right and then to pass by the superbly restored, Queen Anne style Langley Hall. Continue to pass other dwellings on the right and then cross the stile by the signpost on the right to enter a field.

The Hollins

This is a well-used path which was almost certainly used as a route for those who walked from Macclesfield, to work in one of the many early mills in Langley which made good use of the fast flowing waters of the River Bollin. The path dips down to cross the river over the bridge and then curves slightly left as it rises up the next field to a stile beneath a tree. Cross this but you may also like to pause awhile here to take breath and look back over the settlement of Langley.

Head slightly left up the field to a signpost and your way is left along a gorse bank which is often made muddy by the cows which graze this and adjacent fields. It gives out into pasture and you climb a little before levelling and proceeding ahead to a stile at the Hollins, an area well known for its views and opportunities for casual recreation. To the right is a golf course. The path curves right and then left to follow the perimeter fence of the golf course. It then crosses a golf track and bends right to exit onto a road by bungalows by way of a stone step-stile.

Macclesfield

Go left here and then right to walk down an old walled path adjacent to private allotments. The path bends right and passes houses on the left and then houses on the right. Bear left over the bridge and walk down to a junction. Cross over the road and walk through the recreational ground towards the Dolphin pub and St Peter's church. This is Windmill Street, named after a windmill situated here in earlier times. It descends to a bridge over the railway. Go next right after this to pass a number of fine examples of small-scale mills, which hugged the edge of the Bollin. Macclesfield's heritage is silk manufacture and this last section of the walk provides an opportunity to envisage what the town was once like when all of the mills were in production. Keep ahead to walk beneath the Silk Road, an ugly structure which reflects Macclesfield at its worst. Walk along the pavement by the mill and you reach a small footbridge over the river. The building on the right is the home of a locally based micro-brewery, the Storm Brewery, the products of which are sold by several local pubs.

Walk ahead to an area known as Park Green, but at the corner of the mill, there is a narrow thoroughfare on the right, probably dating from medieval times, known as Maydews Passage. This exits onto Brook Street. Cross the road, turn left and then right along George Street, which also has some of the later mills to be built in the area. Take the second junction on the left into Pickford Street, which leads into Sunderland Street, where you bear right for the final walk to Waters Green.

Walk 29. Wildboarclough

The Route: Higher Nabbs, Lower Nabbs Farm, Owlers Bridge, Rose and Crown at Allgreave, Clough Brook.

Distance: 4 miles. Allow 2 hours exclusive of stops.

Start: Lay-by near the Crag Inn, Wildboarclough (Grid reference 981 682).

Map: OS Explorer OL 24 – The Peak District, White Peak Area.

How to get there:

By bus – *There is a summer service 67 at weekends to Wildboarclough from Macclesfield. Ask for The Crag Inn.*

By car – *Travel on the A54 between Congleton-Bosley Crossroads and Buxton. Wildboarclough is signposted off this route. There is a small car park here.*

The Pub

The Rose and Crown at Allgreave (tel: 01260 227232) was a coaching stop on the turnpike road from Buxton. There was a toll house and blacksmith's which have since been incorporated as part of the pub. It dates from 1785 and to this day it provides refreshment to travellers along this rural highway in the Western Peak District. There are two rooms, both offering good views across the surrounding countryside and there are tables set back from the bar. There's also a beer garden to the rear of the pub.

The Rose and Crown is open 11.30am until 3.30pm and from 6.30pm on Mondays to Fridays. It is open all day from 11.00am on Saturdays and Sundays. The cask beers are from Robinson's brewery in Stockport including Robinson's Best Bitter, Frederic Robinson and a seasonal guest beer. Food is usually served between 11.30am and 3.00pm and from 6.30pm to 9.30pm. Families are welcome and overnight accommodation is available (see: www.theroseandcrown.net). This friendly pub welcomes walkers and if you happen to be in a party of six or more seeking food you can give the landlord or landlady a call to say you are coming.

The Walk

This walk does not feature any steep climbs. It starts from The Crag Inn in Wildboarclough, featured in a sister publication 'Best Pub Walks in Cheshire'. Wildboarclough, as the name suggests, is a locality where wild boars once roamed. It is no more than a dispersed hamlet now but this is somewhat deceiving as in the 1950s it was still a thriving mill centre. Workers cottages on the main route through the village were named after their home cities such as Edinburgh and Glasgow. These were subject to the ravages of a raging torrent of water in the late 1990s

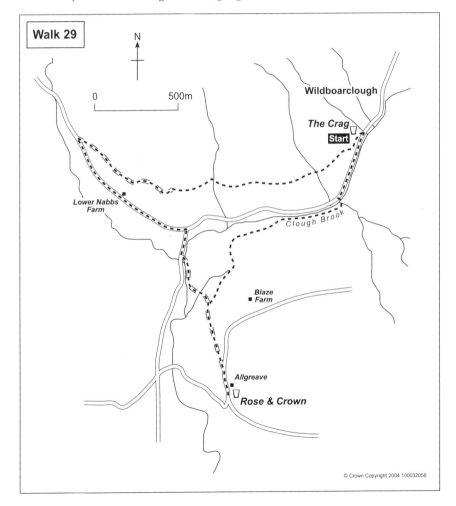

© Crown Copyright 2004 100032058

after a flash flood hit the entire village. On the walk, there are four opportunities to avail yourself to the local produce and beverages of East Cheshire so you had better set a brisk pace to remove any excess calories.

From the entrance to the Crag Inn, go right and at the end of the car park look for a small hinge gate on the right. Go through it and climb the hillside heading slightly right as you pass between maturing hawthorn trees. Just beyond, the path begins to curve more sharply right to another gate (in recent times the gates have replaced stone step-stiles) in a boundary wall. There is a good view behind of the rising ground of Shutlingsloe with its distinctive weathered shape.

Higher and Lower Nabbs

Keep more or less ahead in the next field on a well-trodden path. Go through the gate after the dip and small stream (in wet weather). Go straight on, through the field, again to the small gate. In fact, the line of route is more or less determined by the gates as landmarks. Bear slightly right to the next small gate. Now, keep ahead with an old wall to your left and squeeze through another gate. Pass just to the right of a group of boulders. The farm to the right across the fields is Higher Nabbs. Now bear slightly right to cross a gully and turn left to proceed to a stile next to a gate. Go over it and keep ahead to a gateway near to a dry-stone wall. Go left on the track, through the stile and then climb away from the track to a stile on the right which exits on to a metalled farm access road.

Turn left and follow the road up the valley edge below Piggford Moor. At the junction bear left along the road, which runs down from the Hanging Gate pub to Greenway Bridge and Wildboarclough. It is fairly quiet. Pass through Lower Nabbs Farm and the road then descends to a junction with a dwelling on your right.

The Rose and Crown

At the junction bear right to dip down to a stone bridge which spans a tributary brook flowing into the Clough Brook. Now look for a track on the left that leads to a footbridge, known as Owlers Bridge, across the brook. The track actually runs down to a ford a few metres beyond and hence attracts bikers who fancy a scramble through the sandy banks and shallow water. Once over the bridge go immediately right before the stile and walk along a narrow path to join the track as it rises away from the brook. In very wet weather, the brook rises over this path.

There is an alternative if this happens to be the case when you pass by. Cross the stile into the field and head for a stile just to the right of the building, a camping barn, on the right. Once you are on the track, go right.

However, if all is well and you are on the track, climb up through a small wood to a junction. Keep ahead here for the last stretch up to the main A54 road and The Rose and Crown Inn. Suitably refreshed, retrace your steps to the junction mentioned in the paragraph above. This time continue ahead through the gateway on a concrete track to Underbank and Lower House Cottage. As you approach Underbank there's a treat in store. If you would like farmhouse ice-cream made on the premises or the service of a tea room go right on the permissive path indicated to Blaze Farm, located some 200 metres up the hillside.

Wildboarclough

Anyway, proceeding ahead, you will pass Underbank camping barn and then the green track sweeps right to run alongside Lower House Cottage beneath a wooded hillside. Please pass with consideration. You will see a stile to cross and then in the next field keep company with the wall on the left. It begins to drop down towards the water's edge. Your way is to follow the brook upstream but the path runs at a slightly higher parallel level rather than next to the water's edge. Cross a stile and walk straight on to cross another. The path runs beneath a canopy of trees to a grassy area and the drive of the Brookside Restaurant, another popular haunt for walkers. Turn left to cross the Clough Brook and then walk back along the road to the lay-by and Crag Inn.

Walk 30. Whaley Bridge

The Route: Horwich End, Taxal Church, Taxal Moor, Clayton Fold Farm, Kettleshulme, Kishfield Lane, Slaters Bank Wood, Todd Brook Reservoir.

Distance: 6 miles. Allow 3 hours exclusive of stops.

Start: Whaley Bridge Railway Station (Grid Reference 012815) There is car parking in Whaley Bridge near the canal terminus.

Map: OS Explorer OL 1 – The Peak District, Dark Peak Area and OL 24 – White Peak Area.

How to get there:

By bus –   Daily bus services from Macclesfield (60-64), Buxton and Stockport (199), and New Mills (361).

By train – Daily train service from Buxton and Manchester.

By car –   Whaley Bridge is signposted from the A6 on the A5004 to Buxton.

The Pubs

Be warned, the walk through Whaley Bridge offers temptation. The rambler must have a strong constitution to walk by so many public houses. However, you must visit the Shepherd's Arms.

The Shepherd's Arms at Whaley Bridge (tel: 01663 732840) is a gem of a pub. It concentrates on excellent beer, a warm welcome and good conversation. The pub was originally a farmhouse and pre-dates most of the Victorian buildings surrounding it by several centuries. There are two principal rooms, a comfortable lounge, and the old style tap room with a flagged floor, scrubbed wooden tables and a lovely fire on a winter's day. This type of bar is a rarity these days. There are also plenty of seats in the garden surrounding the pub.

The pub is open on Monday from 4.00pm onwards, Tuesday to Friday from 2.00pm and all day from 12 noon on Saturdays and Sundays. Beers on hand-pull are Marston's Bitter, Pedigree and Banks's Original plus a guest ale. Food is not usually served at this hostelry but can be ordered in advance for parties of walkers. This long-standing CAMRA Good Beer Guide entry can be accessed from the main A5004 main road; it is on the left-hand side in the direction of Buxton – some three minutes walk from the railway station.

The Swan at Kettleshulme

There are also two excellent country pubs to be found half-way along the walk in the village of Kettleshulme. The Bulls Head (tel: 01663 733225), and The Swan (01663 732943), which also happen to be entries in the CAMRA Good Beer Guide, welcome walkers. However, note that on Mondays both are closed at lunchtime. Otherwise, the Swan is open midday until 3.00pm and from 5.30pm onwards whereas the Bull's Head opens from 3.00pm onwards. The pubs are open all day at the weekends. They serve a range of good beers and food is available at lunchtimes from Tuesday to Sunday at The Swan.

The Walk

This walk is moderately strenuous; it has its moments when the climbs become steeper. From Whaley Bridge Railway Station turn right onto the main road and walk through the town centre to pass The Railway Inn, The White Hart and then The Shepherd's Arms. Pass beneath the railway bridge and then, after The Cock Inn, look for a little path on the left, which leads to the old track-bed of the Cromford and High Peak Railway. Go right.

The Cromford and High Peak Railway

The railway, built in the 1830s to link the Peak Forest and Cromford

Canals, was a most unusual affair. It was built by a canal engineer and it
shows. The last section was closed in 1967 and much of the line is now
part of the High Peak Trail. The old railway line stops abruptly at the
development, Cromford Court and you keep right to join New Cross
Road. Bear left for a very short distance along this road and look for a
path leading off right just past a factory. Follow this as it winds up to a
children's play area and keep ahead to go between houses. Go right
along Mevril Road and cross over the main road.

Michael Heathcote

Keep ahead to pass by bungalows to a small gate next to a larger one.
Continue along the track down to the footbridge over the river. The path
becomes a narrow road and climbs alongside the lovely church and
churchyard of Taxal. There's a memorial in the churchyard to Michael
Heathcote, "Gentleman of the pantry and yeoman of the mouth to his
late Majesty King George the Second". Mr Heathcote lived from the late
16th century until 1763, reaching an age of 73, which is remarkable
considering the risks of a food taster especially when sampling for the
monarch of the day.

At the road junction, turn left. Opposite Glebe Farm, go right over a
step-stile by a gate. The way is signposted to Taxal Edge. Walk up to and
cross the stile in the next field boundary and keep ahead to cross two
more gap-stiles. Proceed in a similar direction but there's time to take
stock of the views before crossing another stile and onward to a ladder
stile which exits onto a road.

Taxal Edge

There is a path on the other side of the road through the woodland and
over Taxal Moor but that is not your way today. A far more dramatic
route is followed. Turn left and, at the edge of the wooded area, before
the oaks, look for a well-worn path leading off right, up the hillside by
conifers. This soon becomes a classic green sunken way, curving
upwards to breach Taxal Edge and thus offering exciting views of
Charles Head and surrounding hills. The path leads to a wooden ladder
stile and once over you head slightly right down a pasture to exit on a
road.

Go left and walk along the road to pass a dwelling on the left. The
road dips left to a corner and, at the entrance drive on the right, go right
over the stile into a garden area. The clear path leads to another stile by a

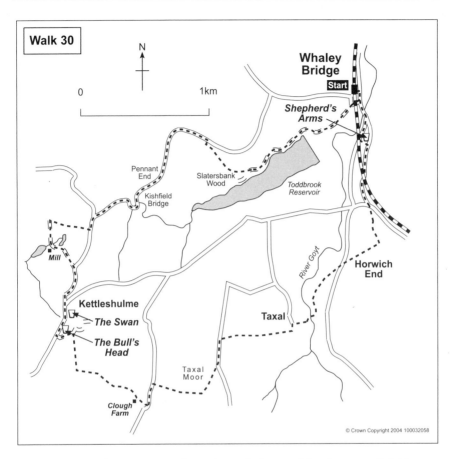

footbridge and gate. Cross the stile and descend in the next field keeping near to the hedge on the right. Go through a barred gate and walk
down the field maintaining a line parallel with the electric telegraph
poles.

The path now dips to cross a stream and then curves up the embankment beneath the farm on the left to a stone step-stile to the right of the
buildings. This leads to a drive. Follow this past a dwelling and then the
track bends right. This exits onto a road in the village. Go left to walk to
the main road where you go right to pass The Bull's Head and then The
Swan.

Lumbhole Mill

Opposite The Swan there is a garden centre and you need to be on that side of the road. Rise up to a corner and at the junction go left into Kishfield Lane. Follow this into the valley and as the road bends by a group of cottages known as Hardy Green, go left along a track, which leads down to Lumbhole Mill. This was a cotton mill dating from the latter part of the eighteenth century. In the nineteenth century, candle-wicks for miners were made here.

The track winds its way past the mill and by a number of dwellings to give out into a field. At this point, go right to walk down to a stile and then a footbridge over the Todd Brook. Rise up the next field to cross a stile. Walk ahead with the hedge to your left until you exit by way of a stile onto Kishfield Lane again.

Go left and descend to a junction. Keep right along the narrow road signed as unsuitable for motor vehicles. That sounds promising. This drops to Kishfield Bridge and now the lane rises up to a place known as Pennant End, shaded by trees with still traditional setts here. It then climbs higher to open countryside and rises to a summit with fine views back to the valley of Todd Brook. The road bends right and passes a number of dwellings. There is a fine collection of roadside flowers on this quiet lane including clover, vetch, harebell and thistle. The road rises again to woodland.

Toddbrook Reservoir

Look out for an isolated post box and a drive down to Salterbrook farm and then Croft Cottage. Be vigilant here for a narrow enclosed path leads off to the right just after the cottage entrance. It passes between gardens to a stile and into Slatersbank Wood. The path winds its way through the woodland to join the top end of Reservoir Road.

Go left to walk along the road which comes near to the reservoir. You can actually get onto a lower path and walk by the water. Either way you reach a dam. The way down is to follow Brookfield Road down past the lodge and by a small nature reserve. This road joins another and you proceed ahead under the railway bridge to the railway station where there are some tantalising smells from the local restaurants and take-aways. Then again, you could always nip back along the main road to step inside The Shepherd's Arms!

Also of Interest

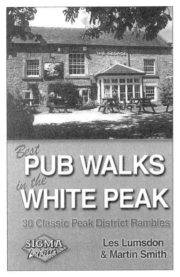

BEST PUB WALKS IN THE WHITE PEAK

Les Lumsdon & Martin Smith

One of our first-ever pub-walk guides and still one of the most authoritative. This book – companion to the Dark Peak title –.covers the White Peak area with its sparkling limestone walls and patchwork of ancient farmland. Regular updates have ensured accuracy. £6.95

ROCKY RAMBLES IN THE PEAK DISTRICT: Geology Beneath Your Feet

Fred Broadhurst

"The Peak District has a dramatic story to tell and Fred Broadhurst is just the guide we need." - Aubrey Manning, presenter of the BBC TV series 'Earth Story'.

With the expert and enthusiastic guidance of Fred Broadhurst, a walk in the Peak District takes on a whole new dimension. Imagine the glaciers, volcanoes and landslips that shaped the Peak District; see for yourself the fossils of ancient plants and animals that were formed beneath its vast seas; find the remains of precious mineral mines. Details and colourful descriptions of where to find them are included in these 18 walks (some circular, full or half-day) with maps, information on parking and refreshments. £7.95

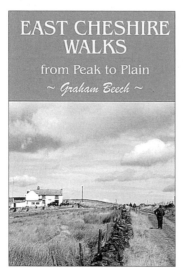

EAST CHESHIRE WALKS
from Peak to Plain: 4th Edition
Graham Beech

Completely checked and revised from cover to cover. The definitive guide to walking in East Cheshire is now in its fourth edition - and is still outselling all other local walking guides! Completely updated and revised, Graham Beech has also added some new walks, including a 20-mile challenge route which offers magnificent views and a real sense of achievement. With 39 walks covering 250 miles, there really is something for everyone! £7.95

PEAK DISTRICT TREASURE
HUNTS: Mystery Tours on Foot & by Car
Ian Almond

If you like a challenge, have good powers of observation, or even fancy your chances at a spot of lateral thinking, you'll not be disappointed. Set in the most scenic hills and quaint villages of the Peak District, these walks offer an intriguing day out. Within each hunt you'll find interesting and varied types of clues to solve – from word searches and grids to code words and calculations. Clues are, in the main, set around fixed items such as plaques, road names, monuments and even headstones. £7.95